Who's on the Menu

For Francesca, a little fatherly extra for someone who was born knowing how to cook, from someone who wasn't.

By the same author

Eating the Alphabet
Who's on the Bottle
Words of Food

Who's on the Menu

The people on your plate

ROBERT BOOTH

BENE FACTUM PUBLISHING

Who's on the Menu

First published in 2014 by
Bene Factum Publishing Ltd
PO Box 58122
London
SW8 5WZ
Email: inquiries@bene-factum.co.uk
www.bene-factum.co.uk

ISBN: 978-1-909657-65-6

Text © Robert Booth

Robert Booth has asserted his right to be identified as Author of this Work in accordance with the Copyright, Designs and Patents Act, 1988.

All rights reserved. This book is sold under the condition that no part of it may be reproduced, copied, stored in a retrieval system or transmitted in any form or by any means, electronic, mechanical, photocopying, recording or otherwise without prior permission in writing of the publisher.

A CIP catalogue record of this is available from the British Library.

Cover and book design by Henry Rivers, thatcover.com
Printed and bound in Great Britain by Clays Ltd, St Ives plc.

Contents

Introduction
9

Snacks and Starters
11

Soup
23

Salads
49

Pizze and Pasta
69

Beef
77

Veal
105

Lamb
115

Pork
123

Game
127

Chicken
139

Eggs
161

Fish
175

Seafood
193

Sauces
213

Vegetables
229

Puddings
241

Sandwiches
255

Acknowledgements
263

Introduction

There was a time not so long ago when, if asked how many dishes named after well-known people there were in the culinary repertoire, I would have found it hard to suggest more than two – Peach Melba and Beef Wellington. However, things changed pretty quickly when the idea for a whole book about who these lucky (or possibly unlucky) celebrities were came to me one day at White's Club in London. I had been invited to lunch there by a noble friend from the club to which we both belonged, the Chelsea Arts. He was a member of both.

On the fairly substantial menu I noticed Sole Véronique, and out loud idly wondered who Véronique might have been. 'Probably a tart,' was my host's somewhat impatient reply, implying that I should have been deciding on what I wanted to eat rather than dreaming about irrelevant details. In spite of the reprimand, however, the identity of Véronique remained a mystery that I was determined to solve, and indeed soon did. As you can read, she was most certainly not what was politely known – at the time when the dish was named after her – as a *grande cocotte*.

After this, as they say, one thing soon led to another, and I found myself discovering a great many people whose names, for one reason or another, had appeared on menus around the world. I hope you will have as much mouth-watering fun reading about them as I had in finding them.

Robert Booth

Editor's note: This is not a cookery book. Many of the recipes scattered throughout are quoted from original sources from across the world as well as various periods. These have been included for the reader's pleasure and interest, rather than the chef's. As a result, there is little consistency with regard to the names of ingredients and units of measurements. But don't let that stop you trying them...

SNACKS AND STARTERS

~

Ham mousseline à la Belmont

A very rich ham and chicken mousse with cream and Madeira.

August Belmont (1816–90) was born in Prussia and emigrated to the US to work for the New York branch of Rothschild's bank. He became extremely wealthy, married the daughter of Commodore Matthew Perry, and was a leading figure in New York society and American horse-racing. **Ham mousseline à la Belmont** was created at Delmonico's by Charles Ranhofer, almost certainly for a dinner given there in Belmont's honour.

Recipe

(From Delmonico's Restaurant in New York)

Chop very fine a pound of cooked ham, and a quarter of a pound of breast of chicken freed from nerves and fat. Add two dessertspoonsful of cold Béchamel Sauce, thickened with cream and eight egg-yolks, and pour in slowly three spoonsful of good cream and one of Madeira. Add the same volume of well drained whipped cream as there is forcemeat, and finish the same as mousseline à la Costa. Serve separately a chicken essence, thickened with rice flour, to which a little tomato purée is added, and some lean ham cut in very small dice.

Bismarck Herring

'There is a Providence that protects idiots, drunkards, children and the United States of America.'

The **Bismarck Herring** is pickled, fresh, filleted Baltic herring, traditionally packed in small wooden barrels.

Otto von Bismarck (1815–98), 'The Iron Chancellor', was the man at the heart of German Unification in 1871.

From his earliest days, gastronomy was Bismarck's ruling passion. In 1878 at the Congress of Berlin, Bismarck apparently presided over the reorganisation of the Balkans by the European 'Great Powers' and the Ottoman Empire while eating pickled herrings with both hands.

Another story relates how, in 1883, when Bismarck was seriously overweight (more than 17 stone, 108 kg), which made him both ill and bad-tempered, in order to do something about this, he lived for several months on a diet of herrings. Thus he made a full recovery and reduced his weight to 14 stone (89 kg).

The story, told by Ed Pierce in *Trivial Biographies*, is, I think, somewhat doubtful. The one below is rather more likely.

Johann Wiechmann had a shop in Stralsund, Germany, where his wife Karoline prepared herring for sale. Wiechmann much admired Bismarck and on Bismarck's birthday (1st April) sent him a barrel of herrings. When the German Empire was created in 1871, Wiechmann sent Bismarck a second barrel, and this time asked if he might name the herrings after him. Bismarck agreed. The original recipe Bismarck Herring were sold from then until the end of World War II, and then revived in 1997.

Carpaccio

A very Venetian starter; very, very thin slices of raw beef served with a Worcestershire-saucy mayonnaise.

Vittore Carpaccio (c. 1465–1525) was a Venetian Renaissance painter.

It was a Venetian contessa, Amalia Nani Mocenigo, a local regular at Harry's Bar in Venice, whose strict diet was the inspiration for the creation of this now classic starter. The countess's doctor had recommended that she only eat raw meat. When she told the founder and owner of Harry's Bar, Giuseppe Cipriani, about this somewhat daunting demand, Cipriani is said to have poured her a drink and asked her to wait for just a few minutes while he disappeared into the kitchen in search of inspiration. Sure enough, Cipriani soon appeared with a dish of paper-thin raw beef crosshatched with his secret 'universal sauce'. This momentous event happened in 1950, the year of what has come to be known as 'The Great Carpaccio Exhibition'. The colour of his raw beef reminded Cipriani of the brilliant reds used by the painter; and so the dish had a name.

Recipe

For about 250 ml of sauce you'll need ¾ of a cup of homemade mayonnaise, 1 or 2 teaspoons of Worcestershire Sauce, 1 teaspoon of fresh lemon juice, 2–3 tablespoons of whole milk, salt and freshly ground white pepper. Put the mayonnaise in a bowl and add the lemon juice and Worcestershire Sauce. Whisk to blend. Add just enough milk to thin the sauce so it is thin enough to just barely coat the back of a wooden spoon. Taste. Add salt and pepper to taste.

Côtelettes de poulet à la Adolphe Hardy

Fried chopped chicken cutlets with ceps.

Adolphe-Marie Hardy (1868–1954) was a Belgian poet and journalist who rose to become a major figure in French literature.

In 1931 Hardy received the *Grand Prix de la langue française* from the Académie Française for his poem *Le Cortège des mois*. He was the first Belgian to win the prize.

Charles Ranhofer (1836–99), the chef at Delmonico's restaurant in New York, honoured Hardy by naming not only a goose liver pâté, *Pâté de filets d'oie Adolphe Hardy*, after him, but also this chicken dish, **Côtelettes de poulet à la Adolphe Hardy**.

Recipe

(From Delmonico's Restaurant in New York)

Chop up finely one pound of raw chicken fillets, after removing all the sinews and fat; add half the same quantity of fresh butter, season and mix the whole well together. Divide the preparation into two inch in diameter balls and shape them like a cutlet; dip them in beaten eggs and breadcrumbs and fry in clarified butter; drain and decorate with paper frills. Arrange them in a circle, filling the centre with a garnishing of minced cèpes fried in butter, drained and moistened with cream reduced with the cèpes. Season and just when ready to serve finish with a piece of butter, lemon juice and chives chopped very fine.

Large, Hot Sweetbread Patty à la McAlister

(Gros pâté chaud de ris de veau à la McAlister)

Veal sweetbreads, chicken forcemeat, Madeira, ham, eggs and truffles, another supremely rich Ranhofer creation. It was served hot.

Samuel Ward McAlister (1827–95) was best known for coining the phrase 'the Four Hundred', which described his list of the 400 people he considered to be New York City society. According to him, 400 was the number of people in New York who really mattered; the people who felt at ease in the ballrooms of high society. 'If you go outside that number,' he warned, 'you strike people who are either not at ease in a ballroom or else make other people not at ease.'[*] The number 400 was popularly supposed to be the capacity of Mrs William Backhouse Astor Jr.'s[†] ballroom.

---

[*] *The Four Million* (1906), a book by O. Henry, was a reaction to this phrase, and expressed Henry's opinion that *every* human being in New York was worthy of notice.

[†] Mrs William Backhouse: Caroline Webster 'Lina' Schermerhorn, '*the* Mrs Astor' or 'Mrs Astor' (1830–1908), was a prominent American socialite, the wife of the businessman, racehorse breeder and owner, and yachtsman William Backhouse Astor Jr. (1829–92). Their son Colonel John Jacob Astor IV perished on the *Titanic*.

Melba Toast

'The first rule in opera is the first rule in life: see to everything yourself.'

Melba Toast is a dry, crisp and thinly sliced toast, often served with soup and salad, or topped with either melted cheese or pâté.

Dame Nellie Melba (1861–1931), born Helen 'Nellie' Porter Mitchell, was an outstanding Australian operatic soprano. She became one of the most famous singers of the late 19th and early 20th centuries and was the first Australian to achieve international recognition as a classical musician.

Melba made her operatic début as Gilda in *Rigoletto* on 12th October 1887 at the Théâtre de la Monnaie in Brussels. The critic Herman Klein described her Gilda as 'an instant triumph of the most emphatic kind…followed…a few nights later with an equal success as Violetta in *La Traviata*.' It was at this time that she adopted the stage name of Melba, from the name of her home city, Melbourne.

Melba Toast is thought to date from 1897 when the singer was very ill and it became a staple of her diet. The toast was created for her by the then chef at the Ritz Hotel in London, Auguste Escoffier. It was the hotel proprietor César Ritz who supposedly named it in a conversation with Escoffier.

See **Peach Melba**, page 247.

Recipe

Melba Toast is made by lightly toasting slices of bread under a grill on both sides. The resulting toast is then sliced in half laterally and the thin slices are returned to the grill with the untoasted sides towards the heat source, resulting in toast half the normal thickness

Nachos

Tortilla chips with cheese and jalapeño peppers, named for **Ignacio 'Nacho' Anaya** (c. 1894–1975), the Mexican restaurateur who is credited with their invention.

Anaya was living and working at Rodolfo De Los Santos' restaurant The Victory Club in Piedras Negras, Coahuila, Mexico, just across the border from Eagle Pass, Texas, USA.

During World War II, wives of American military officers who lived at the Eagle Pass army base would often venture over the Rio Grande to Piedras Negras. On one of these excursions, a group of women stopped at The Victory Club for a bite to eat. While very happy for the business, Ignacio Anaya, who greeted the women, was in a bit of a predicament – he couldn't find the cook. Not wanting to turn away patrons, he 'put on his chef's hat' and, after looking round the kitchen, threw together what he had. According to *The Oxford Companion to American Food and Drink*, this consisted of 'neat canapés of tortilla chips, cheese and jalapeño peppers'.

Nacho Anaya called his creations **Nachos Especiales**. And so thanks to a missing chef, the nacho was born. While they are now often served at Mexican-American restaurants, they're not a typical Mexican dish. They were invented in Mexico but created for an American palate.

Though nachos continued to gain popularity for 20 years after their invention, they only really took off thanks to Frank Liberto, who began to sell them as stadium food at Arlington Stadium (then home of baseball's Texas Rangers). Liberto made one major tweak to Anaya's recipe – because real cheese didn't have a great shelf life (and melting it would need an oven or grill) Liberto devised a fast-food form of Anaya's masterpiece that was part-cheese and part-secret ingredients. The new sauce didn't need to be heated, and when it came to shelf life, it 'could likely survive a nuclear blast'.

Ignacio Anaya died in 1975, aged 81. His son, Ignacio Anaya Jr. lived in Eagle Pass, Texas and gave several interviews about his father, saying that Mamie Finan was the woman who named it 'Nachos Especiales' after being served the snack with several friends.

In the early 1990s, an American holiday called the International Day of the Nacho was initiated to commemorate the invention of nachos and to celebrate nachos in general. It takes place on 21st October, and is observed, not surprisingly, chiefly by eating nachos.

SOUP

~

Consommé Princess Alice

Consommé Princess Alice is a consommé of chicken stock, shredded lettuce, and artichoke bottoms or hearts cooked in butter. It also contains vermicelli and is garnished with chervil.

Princess Alice, Countess of Athlone (1883–1981), was the daughter of Queen Victoria's youngest son Prince Leopold, and Princess Helena of Waldeck-Pyrmont.

Du Barry Cream Soup

(Potage à la du Barry)

This cream of cauliflower soup was a great favourite of **Madame du Barry**; so much so, that if she was served anything other than this as a starter, she would send it back and demand cauliflower soup.

The beautiful Jeanne Bécu, Comtesse du Barry (1743–93), was the last and favourite mistress of King Louis XV. She was guillotined in her fiftieth year on 8th December 1793. She did not go quietly, as had Marie-Antoinette seven weeks earlier; in her last moments Madame du Barry wept and pleaded with the executioner, with the now legendary words, for '*Encore un moment, monsieur le bourreau, un petit moment*'. This was a sad and undignified end for a woman who had begun life as an illegitimate seamstress, but who, thanks to her great beauty, had risen to enjoy a powerful and extravagant life as a courtesan, and the last mistress of Louis XV.

Madame du Barry's name has become associated with a number of dishes based on cauliflower. But why? Perhaps the white cauliflower suggested her fine pale skin, or her powdered wig, or even the design of the wig itself.

Recipe

Boil a medium cauliflower broken into florets in salt water until it is well done but not mushy. Purée it or rub it through a sieve. Mix it with about a quarter of its weight of potato purée. Now add enough chicken or vegetable stock (or milk) until it is of a smooth and creamy consistency. Stir in as much double cream as you dare. Season. Just before serving sprinkle with finely chopped parsley.

Coburg Soup

Coburg Soup is made with chopped Brussels sprouts, onion, and pieces of smoked ham slowly sweated in butter. Everything is then simmered in a rich milky broth. It's served with a splash of sherry and tiny cubes of toast (*sippets*). Traditionally the soup is puréed, which turns it a pale shade of green.

In her book *Cookery and Household Management*, Mrs Beeton recommended deepening the colour with 'green colouring, if needed'.

There are two possibilities as to after whom the soup was named: some say it was created for Queen Victoria's consort, **Prince Albert of Saxe-Coburg** (1819–61), who loved Brussels sprouts; others that it was named after the Queen's oldest son 'Bertie' (1841–1910), who was to become **King Edward VII**.

See **Fillet of Beef Prince Albert** page 78 and **Poularde Edouarde VII**, page 144.

Recipe

1 medium-sized onion, finely chopped
2 medium-sized potatoes, peeled and diced
4 cups of chicken stock

1 tablespoon of sugar
10 oz pack of frozen Brussels sprouts
1½ cups of single cream
¼ of a cup of sherry
2 oz of cooked ham, finely diced
Salt and pepper

Lady Curzon Soup

A turtle soup with sherry.

Lady Curzon, *née* Mary Victoria Leiter (1870–1906), was the wife of the Viceroy of India, Lord George Nathaniel Curzon. She was the daughter of the Chicago businessman Levi Z. Leiter, the co-founder of the original department store which is now called Marshall Field.

Allegedly, around 1905, somewhat mischievously, Lady Curzon directed the inclusion of sherry in her soup when a teetotal guest prevented the usual serving of alcohol at a dinner. Lady Curzon's soup would have been made with green sea turtle meat. The green sea turtle is endangered and is now a protected species.

Hence no recipe.

Soup Fontanges

Soup Fontanges is made with a pea purée in a beef or chicken consommé to which is added sorrel cooked in butter, plus double cream and egg yolk.

Marie Angélique de Scorailles, Duchesse de Fontanges (1661–81), was a French noblewoman, and one of King Louis XIV's many mistresses, coming after Madame de Montespan and before Madame de Maintenon. She was described as *'Belle comme un ange, mais sotte comme un panier'*, or as we might say in English, 'as pretty as a picture but as daft as a brush'.

Although she does have the soup named after her, she is probably better remembered for accidentally creating a hairstyle. One day during a hunt in the forest of Fontainebleau, her hair got caught in the branch of a tree with the result that she appeared before the king with her hair loosely tied in a ribbon and with her curls falling to her shoulders. This rustic style delighted the king, and not surprisingly, the next day all the ladies at court had adopted it. All of them that is, except the obviously miffed Madame de Montespan, who claimed it was in bad taste.

Consommé Garibaldi

A consommé with spaghetti and green olives.

Giuseppe Garibaldi (1807–82) was the foremost military figure and popular hero of the age of Italian unification known as the *Risorgimento*. Along with Cavour and Giuseppe Mazzini, he is thought of as being one of the makers of modern Italy. Cavour is known as the 'brain of unification', Mazzini the 'soul', and Garibaldi the 'sword'. As you might expect, there are numerous edibles named after him. Perhaps the best known among them, apart from Garibaldi squashed fly biscuits, is the **Consommé Garibaldi**.

Recipe

Boil a quarter of a pound of spaghetti, and then cut it into pieces about an inch long. Cut a dozen green queen olives *julienne* style, and add these, with the spaghetti, to three pints of hot consommé. Serve with grated cheese.

Jenny Lind Soup

This is a thick soup made with mashed swede, chicken stock thickened with a *roux*, Gruyère cheese, sago (though some recipes, including one by James Joyce in *Ulysses**, wrongly suggest sage), egg yolks, and double cream. As if that wasn't enough it's topped with beaten egg whites.

Johanna Marie Lind, or **Jenny Lind** (1820–87), was a hugely popular 19th-century singer, known as 'the Swedish Nightingale'. Having announced her retirement at the age of 29 in 1849, the following year she nevertheless went on what became a hugely successful tour of America. Under the management of P.T. Barnum she gave 93 concerts, and then under her own management continued to tour. The tour made her very rich indeed. A great deal of her money she gave to charity. In 1855 Jenny Lind settled in England where she became professor of singing at the Royal College of Music.

A steam train on the London Brighton and South Coast Railway was named after her, as was a tower in Massachusetts and a couple of ships.

---

* In *Ulysses*, Leopold Bloom, while lunching in the Ormond, fantasises: 'Jenny Lind soup: stock, sage, raw eggs, half-pint of cream. For creamy dreamy.'

One of these sank in a creek in Queensland, which, not surprisingly, was soon named the Jenny Lind Creek.

See **Oyster Omelette Jenny Lind**, page 204.

Cream of Cardoon Soup à la Livingstone

'I will go anywhere, provided it is forward.'

This is made with an onion softened in butter, chicken or vegetable stock, lemon juice, Maldon salt, cardoons and double cream.

The encounter, on 10th November 1871, between **Dr David Livingstone** (1813–73) and the journalist and explorer Henry Morton Stanley is legendary. Though we are not sure that Stanley really ever did say 'Dr Livingstone I presume', the phrase must be one of the best known. Less well known is Livingstone's reply: 'Yes. I feel thankful I am here to welcome you.'

Even less well known is the soup named after the great man.

Lord Mayor's Soup

A broth of pig's feet and ears with herbs, thickened, with sherry.

The name obviously begs the question, which Lord Mayor? The original recipe comes from *Modern Cookery for Private Families* by Eliza Acton, first published in 1845. That year the Lord Mayor of London was **John Johnson** from The Worshipful Company of Spectacle Makers. He was the first of some 30 members of the company who have, to date, become Lord Mayor.

Recipe

(From *Modern Cookery for Private Families* by Eliza Acton)

We prefer to have this soup made, in part, the evening before it is wanted. Add the same proportion of water to the ears and feet as in the preceding directions; skim it thoroughly when it first boils, and throw in a tablespoonful of salt, two onions of moderate size, a small head of celery, a bunch of herbs, two whole carrots, a small teaspoonful of white peppercorns, and a blade of mace. Stew these softly until the ears and feet are perfectly tender, and, after they are lifted out, let the liquor be kept just simmering only, while they are being boned, that it may not be too much reduced. Put the bones back into it, and stew them as gently as possible for an hour; then strain the soup into a clean pan, and set it by until the morrow in a cool place. The flesh should be cut into dice while it is still warm, and covered with the cloth before it becomes quite cold. To prepare the soup for table clear the stock from fat and sediment, put it into a very clean stew-pan, or deep saucepan, and stir to it when it boils six ounces of the finest rice-flour smoothly mixed with a quarter of a teaspoonful of cayenne, three times as much of mace and salt, the strained juice of a lemon, three tablespoonsful of Harvey's Sauce, and half a pint of good sherry or Madeira. Simmer the whole for six or eight minutes, add more salt if needed, stir the soup often, and skim it thoroughly; put in the meat and herbs, and after they have boiled gently for five minutes, dish the soup, add forcemeat-balls or not, at pleasure, and send it to table quickly.

Should the quantity of stock exceed five pints, an additional ounce or more of rice must be used, and the flavouring be altogether increased in proportion. Of the minced herbs, two-thirds should be parsley, and the remainder equal parts of lemon thyme and winter savoury, unless sweet basil should be at hand, when a tea-spoonful of it may be substituted for half of the parsley. To some tastes a seasoning of sage would be acceptable: and a slice or two of lean ham will much improve the flavour of the soup. This soup may be rendered very rich by substituting strong bouillon or good veal broth for water, in making it.

Bisque of Shrimps à la Melville

(Bisque de crevettes à la Melville)

---

*'Friendship at first sight, like love at first sight,
is said to be the only truth.'*

This is a rich cream of prawn soup created by the chef at Delmonico's Restaurant in New York, Charles Ranhofer. Although Ranhofer was of French origin, he spent most of his working life in New York, so I am assuming that when he said 'shrimps' he was thinking as an American and referring to what in the UK we call 'prawns'.

I say *potayto*, you say *potahto*, I say *tomayto* you say *tomahto*...

The American writer **Herman Melville** (1819–91) was the author of, among many other things, *Billy Budd* and *Moby Dick*. In 2010 it was announced that a new species of extinct giant sperm whale, *Livyatan melvillei*, had been named in honour of Melville. The palaeontologists who discovered the fossil were all fans of *Moby Dick*.

The huge mammal with which he is associated and the tiny crustacean in the soup make a nice juxtaposition.

Potage anglais de poissons à la Lady Morgan

A soup of fillets of sole, fish quenelles, mushrooms and black truffle arranged on the soup plate to resemble the Union Jack, certainly eccentric, if not delicious.

Sydney, Lady Morgan, *née* Sydney Owenson (1776–1859), was a popular Irish novelist and friend of Sheridan. She is best known as the author of *The Wild Irish Girl*, first published in 1806. It was in Paris in 1829, when Lady Morgan was visiting the banker James Mayer de Rothschild, that the latter's chef, Antoine Carême, created this soup in her honour.

Potage Parmentier

Potage Parmentier smells good, tastes good, and couldn't be simpler to make. It is named for **Antoine-Augustin Parmentier** (1737–1813), the pioneering French expert in nutrition and food chemistry.

See **Potatoes Parmentier**, page 236.

Recipe

- 1 lb of potatoes, washed, perhaps peeled, sliced or diced
- 1 lb of thinly sliced leeks, including the tender green parts
- 4 pints of water
- A teaspoon of salt
- 4 or 5 tablespoons of cream, double or single...
- 2 or 3 tablespoons of chopped parsley or chives

Simmer the vegetables, water, and salt together, partially covered, for 40 to 50 minutes until the vegetables are tender.

Mash the vegetables in the soup with a fork, or pass the soup through a food mill. Correct the seasoning. Set aside uncovered until just before serving, then reheat to the simmer.

Off the heat and just before serving, stir in the cream. Pour into a tureen or soup bowls and decorate with the parsley or chives.

Ronald Reagan's Hamburger Soup

'All great change in America begins at the dinner table.'

A simple soup made with minced beef, butter, onions, garlic, carrots, black pepper, hominy, green peppers, beef broth (made with beef bouillon cubes), chopped celery and chopped tomatoes (tinned or fresh).

Ronald Reagan (1911–2004) was the 40th President of the United States.

There's been speculation that this soup first made news after Reagan innocently announced his liking for fancy French soups and was immediately accused of being elitist. Whatever, it is definitely a homespun, plain soup, and not as bad as you might think when you see that there's hominy in it. This corn product, with its Native American Algonquin name, was an important food to early US pioneers. It is made into a firm, almost dumpling-like little ball in the soup.

Note that the ingredients' non-elitist allowance for tinned foods and bouillon cubes.

Rumford's Soup

Rumford's Soup (1 part pearl barley, 1 part dried (yellow) peas, 4 parts potato, salt, old sour beer) isn't noted for being particularly tasty, but it allegedly becomes thick and palatable with long, slow cooking.

Benjamin, Count von Rumford (1753–1814), was born Benjamin Thompson in Woburn, Massachusetts.

During the American Revolution, having been accused of being loyal to the Crown, he fled to Britain. He went on to have a brilliant career as a scientist, social reformer and inventor. When his work for the Bavarian government earned him the title of Count of the Holy Roman Empire, he chose the name Rumford from the New Hampshire town where he had lived for a time.

His biggest project may have been his plan to rid Munich of its beggar problem by feeding, and more pointedly, employing the poor.

'At the hour of dinner,' Rumford wrote, 'a large bell was rung in the court, when those at work in the different parts of the building repaired to the dining-hall; where they found a wholesome and nourishing repast.' This consisted of 'a very rich soup of peas and barley, mixed with cuttings of fine white bread; and a piece of excellent rye bread, weighing seven ounces, which last they commonly put in their pockets, and carried home for their supper.'

Rumford was also an early proponent of the potato as good, cheap and filling food, though this New World ingredient was still viewed with suspicion by many Europeans (see **Potatoes Parmentier**, page 236).

Although some of his methods (like child labour) wouldn't necessarily go down well today, the basic concept of Rumford's programme set the groundwork for the 19th century's soup kitchens. And through his many scientific innovations, he developed tools that improved cooking for everyone, poor or not, including the first commercially available kitchen range, the cast-iron Rumford Stove (this kept in heat and allowed temperature to be regulated better than on an open hearth), a pressure cooker (though not necessarily the first one), and a drip coffee maker.

But the item bearing Rumford's name that is probably most familiar to cooks today wasn't actually his invention: Rumford Aluminium Free Baking Powder was named in his honour.

Consommé George Sand

'Life resembles a novel more often than novels resemble life.'

This is a consommé garnished with quenelles made from white fish and crayfish. It also contains morilles, and croûtons spread with soft-cooked carp roe.

George Sand is the pseudonym of Amandine-Aurore-Lucile Dupin, Baronne Dudevant (1804–76), a major figure in mid-19th century Parisian society. She was the author not only of 12 plays and 42 novels but of several other volumes of travel and autobiography. She is equally well known for her much publicised romantic affairs with a number of celebrities, including Chopin and Alfred de Musset.

See **Chicken Fricassée George Sand**, page 152.

Consommé Marie Stuart

'In my end is my beginning.'

Beef Consommé Marie Stuart is just that, beef consommé, with marble-sized turnip and carrot balls. It's garnished with parsley or chervil.

Lamb Consommé Marie Stuart has pearl barley and whatever seasonal vegetables there are to hand, cut very small.

They are named for **Marie Stuart**, or Mary Queen of Scots (1542–87). Quite why a soup, let alone two soups, should have been attributed to this unfortunate lady, no one knows. Mary was briefly Queen of France, then Queen of Scotland. During her short and turbulent Scottish reign (1561–68), she was accused of the murder of her second husband, Lord Darnley, then she was abducted and imprisoned, before they were married, by her third husband, Lord Bothwell.

Mary was the first woman to practice golf in Scotland. She caused a scandal when she was seen playing the game at St Andrews within days of her husband Darnley's murder.

Forced to abdicate the Scottish throne in a civil uprising, Mary fled to England, seeking the protection of her Protestant cousin, Queen Elizabeth I. The presence of a rival, female and Catholic sovereign on English soil created a politically volatile situation for Elizabeth, especially as Mary had legitimate claim to the English throne.

After a public trial, Mary was imprisoned in a series of aristocratic houses for 18 years. The discovery of her involvement in the Babington Plot of 1586, in which she was to be freed by her Catholic supporters and Elizabeth assassinated, meant that in 1587, at her cousin's command, Mary was publicly beheaded.

Mary was executed at Fotheringhay Castle, north of Oundle in Northamptonshire. Her last words before the axe fell over her head were: 'Into thy hands, O Lord, I commend my spirit'. Purple thistles still grow on the site of Mary's execution and are nicknamed Queen Mary's Tears.

Chicken Soup Újházi

(Újházi tyúkleves)

A rich Hungarian chicken and vegetable soup traditionally served at weddings and other special occasions.

Ede Újházi (1844–1915) was a Hungarian actor and amateur cook. He was both an excellent dramatic and comic character actor, and pioneer of the realistic school of acting. He also loved cooking for himself and for his fellow actors. Many legends surround his career, but the most memorable is the one about the creation of his chicken soup while visiting a small restaurant in Budapest. When some soup he had been served hadn't measured up to his expectation, Újházi gave instructions to the cook on how to prepare the dish again using a mature chicken, and adding to it various vegetables, garnishes, and noodles. As the result still wasn't quite satisfactory, Újházi told the chef to include a slice of beef to enhance the strength of the soup. The following day Újházi tasted the newly prepared soup and expressed his total satisfaction.

For the last hundred years *Újházi tyúkleves* has been a speciality at the Gundel Restaurant in Budapest.

SOUP

Recipe

(From *Hungarian Cooking*, www.vonmetz.com)

1 large chicken, quartered
½ a pound of minced beef
2 carrots
2 parsnips or white turnips
2 small kohlrabies
1 leek
1 medium onion
2 leafy halves of celery stalks
2 sprigs of parsley
1 clove of garlic
1 small tomato
½ a cup of thinly sliced mushrooms (optional)
5 peppercorns
1 tablespoon of salt
1½ cups of uncooked egg noodles

Wash and clean the pieces of chicken, and put them with the beef in a large cooking pot; cover with cold water to the halfway mark. Add the peppercorns and bring up to boil. Reduce the heat immediately to medium low and spoon off the froth. Cover and simmer until the meat is halfway done.

Clean all the vegetables thoroughly, including onion and garlic; cut up the carrots, turnips, kohlrabies, and skin the tomato. Lay the vegetables and garnishes on the top of the meat; refill the pot to ¾ with water. Sprinkle in the salt. Bring back to simmer and cook until the meat is almost tender, about 45 minutes.

Put a sieve in a large bowl and pour the soup through. Set the broth aside and let it cool.

Discard the celery, parsley, garlic, tomato, leek and peppercorns, and all the skin and bones. Cut the meat and the remaining vegetables into small pieces.

Degrease the broth and correct the seasoning.

Return the meat and vegetables to the pot and pour the broth over. Slowly bring back to simmer again and add in the noodles and the mushrooms. Continue to cook uncovered until the noodles are done.

Serve immediately.

Purée of Wild Ducks Van Buren

'As to the presidency, the two happiest days of my life were those of my entrance upon the office and my surrender of it.'

This, in spite of its name, is a soup. A *mélange* of veal knuckle, roast duck and plenty of butter, it was created by the chef at Delmonico's Restaurant in New York, Charles Ranhofer.

Martin Van Buren (1782–1862), was the 8th US President. Before becoming president, Van Buren had been 8th Vice President and 10th Secretary of State. He was the first US president not to have been of either British or Irish descent, and as all his presidential predecessors had been born before the Revolution, he was the first to be born an American citizen. Yet another claim to fame is that he was the first president not to have spoken English as his first language; his family was originally Dutch.

Martin Van Buren, is said to have been quite a gourmand, with a taste for rich, savoury French cuisine. The soup certainly lives up to Van Buren's epicurean tastes.

Recipe

(From *The Epicurean*, by Charles Ranhofer)

Roast two ducks for eighteen or twenty minutes, remove the fillets, and break up the bones, putting them into a saucepan with a split knuckle of veal and a quarter of a pound of ham, also two cut up tomatoes, and one onion with four cloves in it. Moisten with four quarts of broth, cook for two hours and strain the broth; pound the fillets after removing all the skin, with the same quantity of cooked hominy, and two ounces of butter, dilute this with the broth, season with nutmeg, and heat it up without boiling. Just when ready to serve incorporate into it four ounces of good butter, and beat the broth up well with a spoon, until all the butter is melted; then pour it into a soup tureen with a garnishing of celery cut in dice, and blanched and cooked in some consommé, also quarter inch squares of brioche dried in the oven.

Potage à la Xavier

This is a simple cream soup with chicken which has at least two stories associated with its name. Some sources say that the gourmand **Louis XVIII of France** (1755–1824) invented the soup when he was Comte de Provence, and also known as Louis Stanislas Xavier de France. Others suggest the soup was named after a Basque missionary to Goa and India, **Francis Xavier** (1506–1552).

The gout-suffering associate of Talleyrand would seem a more likely candidate than a 16th-century Christian missionary.

Recipe

(From the *Larousse Gastronomique*)

Prepare 1½ litres of chicken consommé. Thicken it with 3 tablespoons of rice flour slaked with milk or water. Away from the heat, add 3 egg yolks mixed with 6 tablespoons of double cream. Stir in 2oz of butter. Garnish with diced Chicken Royale [see below].

Chicken Royale

Poach 2oz of white chicken meat and pound it finely. Add 2 tablespoons of **Béchamel Sauce** (page 217) and the same amount of cream. Press it through a sieve. Bind with 4 egg yolks and cook in a *bain-marie* in the oven at 200ºC, 400ºF for half an hour.

SALADS

Caesar Salad

The **Caesar Salad** was invented on 4th July 1924 by **Cesare Cardini** (1896–1956) at Caesar's Palace, his restaurant in Tijuana, northern Mexico. Prohibition was in force in America, and on this particular Independence Day, rather more people turned up at Caesar's Palace than Cardini had expected. Guests included Clark Gable, Jean Harlow and W.C. Fields. But they didn't only want to drink. Cardini soon realised that his supply of fresh vegetables wasn't going to be enough. Inspiration was needed, and was soon found. Luckily Cardini wasn't short of cos lettuce, eggs, lemons, bread or garlic-flavoured olive oil.

Apart from the youthfulness of Jean Harlow* at the time (she was just 13), there is no real reason to disbelieve the legend.

However, George Leonard Herter, in his book *Bull Cook and Authentic Historical Recipes and Practices*, offers another candidate:

'Caesar salad was invented in about 1903 by **Giacomo Junia**, an

---

* Clark Gable was born on 1st February 1901, so he was 23. Jean Harlow on 3rd March 1911, so she was 13, and W.C. Fields on 29th January 1880, making him 44.

Italian cook in Chicago, Illinois. Giacomo Junia was the cook in a small restaurant called The New York Cafe. He catered to American tastes, as spaghetti and pizza in those days were little eaten by anyone, including Italians. It is sometimes falsely stated that this salad was invented in Tijuana, Mexico during the prohibition period and also in San Francisco. Nothing could be further from the truth. The only thing invented in Tijuana were the finest methods ever produced to clip tourists.'

The story of how the dish crossed the pond from America comes from Terry D. Greenfield in his book *In Search of Caesar, The Ultimate Caesar Salad Book*:

'The legend attributes the salad's debut across the ocean to Mrs Wallis Warfield Simpson, mistress and ultimately wife of Prince Edward VIII of Wales, former King of England [sic]. Mrs Simpson often visited and partied in the San Diego and Tijuana areas in the 1920s. It is said that Mrs Simpson met the Prince of Wales there, at the Hotel Del Coronado. During this time, Mrs Simpson visited Hotel Caesar's Palace and became fond of Caesar's Salad, and was sometimes an overbearing guest, demanding that Caesar himself toss his salad at her table-side, creating quite a fuss. It is also as a result of Mrs Simpson's extensive world travels that Caesar Salad was introduced.'

Carmen Salad

Bizet's opera **Carmen**, after which this salad is named, was first performed on 3rd March 1875 at the Théâtre National de l'Opéra-Comique in Paris.

The libretto was by Henri Meilhac and Ludovic Halévy, based on a novella of the same title by Prosper Mérimée. Though today *Carmen* is one of the most frequently performed operas, its first run was of only 36 performances. Sadly Bizet didn't live to see the end of the first run, let alone its huge subsequent success.

Habanera and *Toreador Song* are perhaps the opera's most celebrated arias.

See **Eggs in a Mould Bizet**, page 167.

Recipe

(From Olya Korolevich)

For four

  4 red peppers
  300 g of chicken (boiled fillet)

250 g of green peas
1 cup of rice
4 tablespoons of black olives, pitted
½ a cup of olive oil
1 tablespoon of vinegar
1 teaspoon of mustard
Salt
Parsley

Bake the pepper, cut it in half lengthwise, cleaned of seeds and peel. Remove the chicken skin and cut the meat into strips. Cut the olives into rings. Boil the rice in salted water. For the dressing mix together the oil, salt, vinegar and mustard. Mix the rice, vegetables, chicken and add with dressing. When serving, put the salad in the pepper halves and decorate with the parsley.

Two other possibilities exist: one with lettuce, salted cashew nuts, noodles, water chestnuts and salted sunflower seeds; the other with lettuce, red onion and either sliced strawberries or mandarin orange sections, or even both.

Cobb Salad

The **Cobb Salad** is an American salad made from chopped salad greens (iceberg lettuce, watercress, endives, and Romaine lettuce), tomato, crisp bacon (grilled or roasted, but not fried) chicken breast, hardboiled egg, avocado, chives, Roquefort cheese, and red-wine vinaigrette. Black olives are also often included. One way to remember the components is to use the mnemonic 'EAT COBB': Egg, Avocado, Tomato, Chicken, Onion, Bacon, Blue cheese. Sadly this misses out the watercress, endives and vinaigrette, and you have to remember here that onion means chives.

There are two stories about the invention of the salad. The first credits the executive chef at the Hollywood Brown Derby restaurant, Robert Kreis. He is said to have created the salad in 1929, the year the restaurant opened, and to have named it in honour of the restaurant's owner, **Robert Howard Cobb** (d. 1970).

The second story recounts how, at nearly midnight one evening in 1937, Cobb, very hungry, having not eaten anything all evening, mixed together leftovers he found in the kitchen, along with the restaurant's French Dressing and some bacon cooked by his chef, Chuck Wilson.

The salad soon became a signature dish at the Hollywood Brown Derby.

Salade à la Dumas

'All generalizations are dangerous, even this one.'

Alexandre Dumas (1802–70), born Dumas Davy de la Pailleterie, also known as Alexandre Dumas, *père*, was a writer, one of the most widely read of all French authors. Perhaps his best known books are *The Count of Monte Cristo* and *The Three Musketeers*.

With the election of Louis-Napoléon Bonaparte in 1851, Dumas rather fell from favour, and so left France for Belgium, where he stayed for several years. On leaving Belgium, Dumas moved to Russia, before going to Italy. There in 1861, he founded and published the newspaper, *L'Indipendente*, which supported Italian unification. In 1864 he returned to Paris.

Recipe

For two

  1 hardboiled egg yolk
  Chervil
  Tinned tuna
  Chopped anchovy

Chopped gherkins
The chopped white of a hardboiled egg
Vinegar
A pinch of paprika
Oil
Salt and pepper

Put the egg yolk in a salad bowl and make it into a paste with the oil. To this add the chervil, tuna, anchovy, gherkins and egg white. Taste and see if it needs salt and pepper. Add the vinegar. Toss everything together and finally, as the original French recipe suggests 'drop a pinch of paprika onto it from a great height.'

Salade Olivier

Lucien Olivier (1838–83) was a Russian chef of Belgian origin. In the early 1860s he was the owner of the celebrated Hermitage restaurant in the centre of Moscow. He is best known for the creation of **Salade Olivier**. Olivier never disclosed the recipe. He died in Moscow in 1883 at the age of 45 and took the secret of his recipe with him to his grave.

Today, however, this salad has numerous variations, which are a mixture of every ingredient Olivier was known to have used, as well as others that he didn't, plus a mayonnaise dressing. Now it is found around the world, and commonly called Russian Salad.

It is known that the original salad did contain grouse, veal tongue, caviar, lettuce, crayfish tails, capers, and smoked duck, although it is possible that the recipe was varied seasonally.

Salade Rachel

Made with potatoes, Jerusalem artichokes cut into *julienne* strips and asparagus tips dressed with a light mayonnaise.

Mademoiselle Rachel, Elisa-Rachel Félix (1821–58), was a distinguished classical French actress.

Rachel never married; she did however have love affairs with some of the most important men in mid-19th-century France. They included the Prince de Joinville (the son of King Louis-Philippe), **Count Alexandre-Colonne Walewski** (the illegitimate son of Napoleon I by the Polish countess Marie Walewska), the future emperor Louis Napoleon, his cousin Prince Napoleon, the poet Alfred de Musset, and the journalist Emile de Girardin.

Half a dozen distinguished lovers and five dishes named after her – not bad really.

See **Tournedos Rachel**, page 95, **Eggs Rachel**, page 174, **Filets de Sole Rachel**, page 187, **Vegetables Rachel**, page 237, and the **Rachel Sandwich**, page 258.

Salade Réjane

A spicy salad made with rice, hardboiled eggs, grated horseradish, truffles and *crème fraîche*.

Gabrielle Réjane was the stage name of the French actress Gabrielle-Charlotte Reju (1856–1920).

She was born in Paris, the daughter of an actor, and became a pupil of Régnier at the Conservatoire, where in 1874 she took the second prize for comedy. Her début was made the next year, during which she played a number of light, especially *soubrette*, parts. Her first great success was in 1883, in Henri Meilhac's *Ma camarade*. She soon became known as an emotional actress of rare gifts, notably in *Décor*, *Germinie Lacerteux*, *Ma cousine*, *Amoureuse* and *Lysistrata*.

Her most famous role was as Catherine in Sardou's *Madame Sans-Gêne*. Her performances in the play made her as well known in England and the United States as in Paris. In later years she appeared in characteristic parts in both countries, being particularly successful in *Zaza* and *La Passerelle*. She opened the Théâtre Réjane in Paris in 1906.

Along with her great rival, Sarah Bernhardt, she served as the model for the character of the actress Berma in Marcel Proust's novel *In Search of Lost Time*. During the early years of cinema, Réjane appeared in several short films, including, in 1908, an experimental sound film.

In 1892 she married the director of the Théâtre du Vaudeville, Paul Porel, but the marriage was dissolved in 1905. She became a knight of the *Legion d'honneur* three months before her death in Paris on 14th June 1920.

See **Paupiettes Réjane**, page 188.

Salad Sydney Smith

'Madam, I have been looking for a person who disliked gravy all my life; let us swear eternal friendship.'

Sydney Smith (1771–1845) was an English writer, wit, Anglican clergyman, and founder of *The Edinburgh Review*.

In the 18th, 19th and early 20th centuries, rhyming recipes were a popular way for people to remember recipes. Today one of the best known is Sydney Smith's:

> *Two boiled potatoes strained through a kitchen sieve,*
> *Softness and smoothness to the salad give;*
> *Of mordant mustard take a single spoon,*
> *Distrust the condiment that bites too soon!*
> *Yet deem it not, thou man of taste, a fault*
> *To add a double quantity of salt.*
> *Four times the spoon with oil of Lucca crown,*
> *And twice with vinegar procured from town;*
> *True taste requires it and your poet begs*
> *The pounded yellow of two well-boiled eggs.*
> *Let onion's atoms lurk within the bowl*
> *And, scarce suspected, animate the whole,*
> *And lastly in the flavoured compound toss*
> *A magic spoonful of anchovy sauce.*
> *Oh, great and glorious! Oh, herbaceous meat!*
> *'Twould tempt the dying Anchorite to eat,*
> *Back to the world he'd turn his weary soul*
> *And plunge his fingers in the salad bowl.*

Yet other rhyming recipes still exist. From *Favorite Recipes* (1923) comes Dr Laura Dice's recipe for Rice Pudding:

> *One quart of milk to make it nice,*
> *Only nine teaspoonsful of rice,*

Nine teaspoonsful of sugar too,
Also a pinch of salt mixed through;
Two teaspoonsful of any flavour
Of which you wish the dish to savour.
I, by my own idea possessed,
Consider lemon is the best.
Bake for two hours – not fast nor slow,
But in a moderate oven, so
When it is done, it ought to seem
Thick as the richest kind of cream.

And from *The Cook Book of Left-Overs* (1920), by Mabel E. Sturtevant, here is Mrs Theo Barger's Homely Hash:

One quart of scraps –
Beef, veal, perhaps,
Or pork, or lamb will do.
Pour water over
To barely cover;
Add salt and pepper, too.
When this boils down
And gets quite brown,
Add two large spoons of flour.
Then let it cook
(So runs the book)
A quarter of an hour.
Now toast some bread,
And on it spread

The hash – a dainty brown;
Then eat away!
You'll surely say
It's the best meat in town.

And a recipe for a Sally Lunn, from *The Monthly Magazine* of 1796:

RECEIPT TO MAKE A SALLY LUN
A well-known cake at Bath
Written by the late Major Drewe, of Exeter

No more I heed the muffin zest
The Yorkshire cake or bun
Sweet Muse of Pastry teach me how
To make a Sally Lun.

Take thou of luscious wholesome cream
What the full pint contains
Warm as the native Mood which glows
In youthful virgin's veins

Hast thou not seen in olive rind
The wall-tree's rounded nut
Of juicy butter just its size
In thy clean pastry put

Hast thou not seen the golden yolk
In Chrystal shrine immur'd

Whence brooded o'er by sostring wing
Forth springs the warrior bird?

Oh save three birds from savage man
And combat's sanguine hour
Cush in three yolk, the seeds of life
And on the butter pour

Take then a cup that hold the juice
Fam'd China's fairest pride
Let foaming yeast its concave fill
And froth adown its side

But seek thou first for neatness sake
The Naiad's crystal stream
Swift let it round the concave play
And o'er the surface gleam

Of salt more keen than that of Greece
Which cooks not poets use
Sprinkle thou then with sparing hand
And thro the mass diffuse

Then let it rest disturb'd no more
Safe in its steady feat
Till thrice Time's warning bell hath struck
Nor yet the hour compleat

And now let Fancy revel free
By no stern rule confin'd
On glittr'ing tin in varied form
Each Sally-Lun be twin'd

But heed thou west to lift thy thought
To me thy power divine
Then to the oven's glowing mouth
The woud'rous work consign.

And finally, a 21st-century rhyming recipe by the poet Kit Wright:

If you're no good at cooking
Can't fry or bake,
Here's something you
Can always make. Take
Three very ordinary
Slices of bread.
Stack the first
On the second one's head
Stack the third
On top of that.
There! Your three slices
Lying pat.
So what have you got?
A BREAD SANDWICH
That's what!
Why not?

SALADS

Salad Tosca

Puccini's opera ***Tosca*** was first performed at the Teatro Costanzi in Rome on 14th January 1900. It was based on Victorien Sardou's play *La Tosca* (1887). In spite of receiving indifferent reviews, *Tosca* was an instant success with the public and has been, understandably, hugely popular ever since.

Recipe

For four

- 2 cooked chicken breasts
- 4 celery stalks
- 50 g of mild parmesan
- 1 tablespoon of mayonnaise
- 1 tablespoon of white wine vinegar
- ½ a tablespoon of mustard
- A scant ½ tablespoon of anchovy paste
- About 50 g of extra virgin olive oil
- 1 small white truffle (optional)

First cut the chicken breasts into *Julienne* strips and put them into a bowl. Cut the parmesan in the same way and add it to the chicken. Wash and dry the celery and remove any thick strands. Cut it into strips as you did the parmesan and chicken. Add it to the bowl. Pour the mayonnaise into another bowl and add the olive oil. In a third bowl, mix the mustard, anchovy paste and vinegar; work the mixture with a fork until it's is smooth. Now add this to the olive oil and mayonnaise and mix well.

Just before serving, pour the dressing on the chicken, celery and parmesan. Mix well, and if using a truffle, thinly slice it on now. You might just like to add a pinch of salt.

Waldorf Salad

A **Waldorf Salad** is a salad generally made of apples, celery and walnuts, dressed in mayonnaise, and usually served on a bed of lettuce as an appetiser or a light meal.

It was first created between 1893 and 1896 at the Waldorf Hotel in New York City – owned by **William 'Willy' Waldorf Astor, 1st Viscount Astor** (1848–1919) – the precursor of the Waldorf-Astoria Hotel, which came into being with the merger of the former with the adjacent Astoria Hotel in 1897.

The *maître d'hôtel* at the Waldorf, Oscar Tschirky, developed or inspired many of its signature dishes, and is widely credited with creating the recipe. In 1896, Waldorf Salad appeared in *The Cook*

Book by 'Oscar of the Waldorf'. The original recipe didn't contain nuts, but they had been added by the time the recipe appeared in 1928 in *The Rector Cook Book*.

The salad leapt to fame with its appearance in the episode of *Fawlty Towers*, first broadcast on 1979, in this classic scene:

Mr Hamilton: Would you make me a Waldorf Salad?

Basil Fawlty: [*having never heard of it*] I beg your pardon?

Mr Hamilton: Get me a Waldorf Salad.

Basil Fawlty: Well, I think we just ran out of Waldorfs!

PIZZE

AND

PASTA

~

Fettucine Alfredo

Noodles with butter, cream and parmesan.

Alfredo di Lelio (1880–1959) was a Roman restaurateur.

The story behind his Fettucine all started in 1914 when Alfredo's wife Ines was pregnant with their first child. Her husband, concerned about her health, did everything to make her strong and healthy. It was then that the idea of the dish that eventually became famous around the world was born.

Alfredo prepared noodles mixed with butter, cream and fresh parmesan. He then said a prayer to Saint Anna (protector of pregnant women, whose feast day falls on 26th July) and served the dish to Ines saying: 'If you don't like it, I'll have it.' Ines ate it with great enthusiasm, and then suggested adding it to the menu at their small restaurant.

A decisive step in **Fettucine Alfredo**'s path to success was when, on their honeymoon in Rome in 1920, the two famous American silent film actors, Douglas Fairbanks and Mary Pickford, tasted Alfredo's delicious and original dish at his restaurant in Via della Scrofa. To thank Alfredo for his warm and friendly welcome, the newlyweds gave him a solid gold spoon and fork engraved: 'To Alfredo, the King of the noodles'.

February 7th is National Fettucine Alfredo Day in America (where else?).

Macaroni Lucullus

Macaroni with truffles and *foie gras*. Simple but rich and delicious.

Lucius Licinius Lucullus (c.106–56 BC) was a politician of the late Roman Republic, known for his decadence and appetite. So famous did Lucullus become for his banqueting that the word 'lucullan' now means lavish, luxurious and gourmet.

Once, Cicero and Pompey succeeded in inviting themselves to dinner with Lucullus, but, curious to see what sort of meal Lucullus ate when alone, forbade him to communicate with his slaves regarding any preparation of the meal for his guests. However, Lucullus outsmarted them, and succeeded in getting Pompey and Cicero to allow that he specify in which room he would be dining. He ordered that his slaves serve him in the Apollo Room, knowing that his service staff was schooled ahead of time as to the specific details of service he expected for each of his particular dining rooms. As the standard amount specified to be outlaid for any given dinner in the Apollo room was the large sum of 50,000 drachmas, Cicero and Pompey found themselves a short time later dining upon a most unexpectedly luxurious meal.

On another occasion, so the story goes, his steward, hearing that he would have no guests for dinner, served only one not especially impressive course. Lucullus reprimanded him saying, 'Did you not know that today Lucullus dines with Lucullus?'

Lucullus was responsible for bringing a species of sweet cherry and the apricot to Rome, developing major facilities for aquaculture, and being the only person in Rome with the ability to provide thrushes for gastronomic purposes in every season, having his own fattening coops.

Among the various edible plants associated with Lucullus is a cultivar of the vegetable Swiss chard (*Beta vulgaris*), which is named *Lucullus* in his honour.

Pizza Margherita

This is the simplest, and almost certainly the most popular pizza – tomato, mozzarella and basil. It's believed to be named after **Queen Margherita of Italy** (1851–1926).

In 1889, despite having been united with northern Italy in 1861 by the swashbuckling general Giuseppe Garibaldi, southern Italy was still smarting from its loss of independence. Consequently, that year the Italian king and queen decided to make a visit to Naples, the former capital of the Kingdom of the South, to ingratiate themselves with their southern subjects.

Legend has it that the queen, while staying in Naples' Capodimonte Palace, got sick of the French gourmet food that was the royal standard across Europe at the time. So she summoned the most famous pizza-maker in Naples, Raffaele Esposito, and had him bake her three pizzas in the palace kitchen. Margherita didn't like the one with garlic (Pizza Marinara) or anchovies (Pizza Napoli), but she loved the pizza with tomato sauce, mozzarella and a sprig of basil.

Esposito immediately named his invention after the queen, and asked only to put the royal seal on his pizza.

A few days later she had her chamberlain send Esposito a thank you note, one that hangs to this day on the wall of the Pizzeria Brandi, which his descendants still own.

At least that's the story …

Pasta à la Norma

Spaghetti with aubergines and tomato.

Norma is a *tragedia lirica* or opera in two acts by Vincenzo Bellini with libretto by Felice Romani after *Norma, ossia L'infanticidio* (Norma, or The Infanticide) by Alexandre Soumet. It was first produced at La Scala in Milan on 26th December 1831.

Salad Norma originated in Sicily, as did the composer Vincenzo Bellini. The legend is that the salad (and indeed **Pasta à la Norma**) was created as a tribute to the opera. The opera's most splendid, stirring and best known aria is *Casta Diva*, sung by the Druid High Priestess, Norma.

Recipe

(From Kyle Phillips)

For six

- 6 medium sized aubergines, about 1 lb (500 g)
- 3 garlic cloves, peeled and chopped
- About 1 lb (500 g) of sun-ripened plum tomatoes, blanched, peeled

and chopped.
6–8 basil leaves, shredded
1 lb (450 g) of spaghetti
½ a cup of grated pecorino romano, salted ricotta, or parmesan
Salt and pepper to taste
Olive oil

Peel and slice the aubergines into half-inch (1 cm) slices, salt the slices, and let them sit in a colander for about an hour. Rinse them, pat them dry, and fry them a few pieces at a time in hot oil, turning them so both sides brown, and setting them to drain on absorbent paper.

Next, set water to boil, and while it's heating, heat ¼ of a cup of oil in a pot, sauté the garlic briefly, and then stir in the blanched, peeled tomatoes. Season with salt and lots of pepper to taste. Reduce the heat to a simmer and continue cooking the sauce for 15–20 minutes. About 5 minutes before it's done, add the basil.

Keep an eye on the pasta pot while preparing the sauce, and as soon as the water boils salt it and cook the spaghetti.

When the spaghetti is *al dente*, drain it and season it with the tomato sauce, and then carefully mix in the slices of eggplant. Sprinkle the pasta with much of the cheese, and serve it with the remaining cheese on the side.

BEEF

~

Fillet of Beef Prince Albert

The king of beef cuts, fit for a prince.

Though there may be some doubt about whether **Coburg Soup** (page 26) was named after Queen Victoria's consort or her son, this dish was most definitely named after **Prince Albert** (1819–61).

Recipe

(From the BBC)

- 3 tablespoons of sunflower oil
- 1 medium onion, peeled and sliced
- 1 garlic clove, finely chopped
- 2 medium carrots, peeled and diced
- 2 celery sticks, thinly sliced
- 1 kg of centre cut beef fillet, well-trimmed
- 75 g pack smooth duck liver pâté
- ½ a teaspoon of truffle oil (optional)
- 6–8 thick rashers rindless streaky bacon
- 3 or 4 bay leaves

100 ml of Cognac
200 ml of Madeira
150 ml of fresh beef stock
Flaked sea salt and fresh ground black pepper

Heat two tablespoons of the oil in a frying pan. Fry the onion, garlic, carrots and celery for 10–12 minutes, or until softened and golden-brown. (You may need to increase the heat towards the end of the cooking time to encourage the vegetables to brown.) Spoon the cooked vegetables into a casserole dish.

Put the beef fillet onto a chopping board. Cut a pocket in the side of the fillet, leaving a 2 cm/1 in gap at each end. (Make sure that you only make an incision halfway into the meat and that you don't cut the meat into two pieces).

Cut the pâté into 1.5 cm/½ inch wide strips, put them inside the pocket and drizzle with the truffle oil, if using. Close the pocket to encase the filling. Season the beef all over with sea salt and plenty of freshly ground black pepper.

Wrap the beef in the bacon rashers and secure with kitchen string. Put a bay leaf between the bacon and string every other rasher. Set aside.

Preheat the oven to 180°C/350°F/Gas Mk 4.

Heat the frying pan and add the remaining oil and brown the beef fillet in the frying pan for 10–12 minutes, or until the bacon is crisp and golden-brown. Put the beef fillet on top of the vegetables.

Remove all but two tablespoons of fat from the frying pan and stir in the flour. Slowly add the cognac, stirring constantly. Once the mixture is boiling, add the Madeira, followed by the beef stock. Bring the liquid to a simmer then pour immediately around the beef. Cook the beef in the oven for 30–35 minutes for rare beef, or 40 minutes for medium-rare.

Carefully remove the beef onto a chopping board, cover with a piece of foil and two tea towels. Return the casserole to the hob and simmer for 2–3 minutes, or until the liquid thickens slightly. Strain through a fine sieve into a warmed jug. Carve the beef into thick pieces.

Pour some of the sauce into six deep plates.

Put the beef on top and garnish with fresh parsley and serve with creamed potatoes and green beans.

Chaliapin Steak

A Japanese version of steak with onions. In 1936, when staying at the Imperial Hotel in Tokyo, **Feodor Chaliapin** asked for a tender steak. The chef at the Imperial produced a steak topped with onions that had been reduced and caramelised with Japanese seasonings, and cut with rice vinegar. Chaliapin was delighted, and so apparently, was the hotel, which promptly put it on their menu.

Feodor Chaliapin (1873–1938) was born in Kazan in eastern European Russia, the son of a clerk. As a young man he was apprenticed first to a cobbler, then to a lathe turner. He also worked as a copyist. Though he had very little formal education and little early musical training, his talent led to his taking, in his teens, leading roles with a touring opera company. He had débuts in Saint Petersburg in 1894 and Moscow in 1896, where he played the role he would be most associated with, Boris Godunov. These led to his triumphant début as Mefistofele at La Scala in 1901. His imposing stage presence and fine acting gave him a popularity second only to that of Enrico Caruso.

Decades after his death, Chaliapin is still considered Russia's greatest opera singer. The dynamism of his acting perfectly complemented his voice, which, being a bass, was best suited for the role of the villain. In this Chaliapin (who for the most part was self-taught) created such memorable characters on stage as Mephistopheles in Gounod's *Ivan the Terrible*, the title role in *Boris Godonov* by Mussorgsky, and Holofernes in *Judith* by Aleksandr Serov.

Chateaubriand Steak

The traditional **Chateaubriand** recipe uses a 4- or 5-inch section of beef fillet, one of the tenderest cuts of beef. Because it is so thick, the beef must be roasted carefully to ensure it is properly cooked.

Classically, the Chateaubriand was served with a Chateaubriand Sauce, essentially a variant on the Bercy Sauce (shallots and white wine), but with the addition of lemon juice, tarragon and possibly mushrooms.

Modern Chateaubriand is also often served with a **Béarnaise Sauce** (see page 214).

François-René, Vicomte de Chateaubriand (1768–1848) was a French writer, politician, diplomat, historian and food enthusiast. He is considered to have been the founder of Romanticism in French literature. He was descended from an old aristocratic family from Brittany, and was a royalist by political disposition. In an age when a significant part of the intelligentsia was turning against the Church, he wrote *Génie du christianisme* in defence of the Catholic faith. However it is his autobiography, *Mémoires d'outre-tombe* (Memoirs from Beyond the Grave), published posthumously, which nowadays is considered to be Chateaubriand's most accomplished work.

The Chateaubriand Steak was created by his personal chef, Montmireil.

Delmonico Steak

Delmonico Steak, or if you prefer, Steak Delmonico, refers to a method of preparation from one of several cuts of beef made by **Delmonico's Restaurant** in New York City during the mid-19th century.

There is controversy as to exactly which cut of steak was originally used. There are at least eight different cuts which are claimed to be the original. According to some sources, the original Delmonico Steak was a boneless top sirloin, almost two inches thick, with delicate marbling and cooked to the preference of the diner.

Delmonico's Steak may nowadays refer to other cuts, prepared differently in different parts of the USA. This wider variety of beef cuts may be broiled, fried, or grilled. Some of the steak cuts now commonly referred to as Delmonico Steak include:

- **Boneless rib-eye steak**: this consists of two heart cuts of rib-eye tied together with butcher's twine. It resembles a *filet mignon* in appearance, but because of the more marbled nature of a rib-eye, is more moist. The modern rarity of the Delmonico cut of rib-eye may be due to the fact that it renders the remaining pieces of rib-eye unsaleable as anything but stewing steak, and the profit to be made from a pair of choice rib-eyes is almost always more than that of a single Delmonico. The Delmonico Steak currently served at Delmonico's in New York is a boneless rib-eye.

- **Bone-in top loin steak**: a triangular-shaped, short loin cut (some suggesting the first cut of the top loin next to the rib end), also known as a club steak, country club steak, shell steak, and strip loin steak.

- **Boneless top loin strip steak**: also known as a New York strip steak, Kansas City steak, strip loin, ambassador, boneless club, hotel or veiny steak.

As well as the steak, the original meal also included a potato dish, known as Delmonico's Potatoes, a mashed potato dish topped with grated cheese and buttered breadcrumbs, baked until golden brown, and served steaming.

Steak Esterházy

A spicy steak with mushrooms.

Prince Paul Anton III Esterházy de Galántha (1786–1866) was a Hungarian aristocrat, diplomat and, in 1848, foreign minister. Thanks to his huge landholdings he was enormously rich.

In the 1840s Esterházy visited England, and was a guest of one of England's wealthiest landowners, the 2nd Earl of Leicester, at Holkham Hall. While looking at his beautiful flock of 2,000 sheep, Lord Leicester asked Esterházy if he could show as fine a flock on his estates in Austria. The wealthy baron smiled and replied, 'My shepherds are more numerous than your sheep.' This was absolutely true: Esterhazy had 2,500 shepherds.

Recipe

For two

- ¼ of a pound of mushrooms; diced
- 1 carrot; small, diced
- 1 shallot
- 2 tablespoons of butter

1 teaspoon of paprika
½ a teaspoon of salt
1 cup of sour cream
1 teaspoon of Worcestershire Sauce
2 steaks

Sauté the mushrooms, carrot, and shallot in butter. Add paprika, salt, sour cream, and Worcestershire Sauce. Simmer for 2 minutes. Do not boil. Grill the steaks; top them with the sauce.

Baron of Beef à la Saint George

(Selle de bœuf à la Saint George)

What better day on which to enjoy some roast beef than on Saint George's Day, 23rd April?

The Worshipful Company of Carpenters*, however, enjoy their beef in November. Every November, at their Livery Dinner, they have 'The Ceremony of the Roast Beef'. This is the traditional offering of a **Baron of Beef** to the guests before it is served. The beef is paraded around the room to a musical accompaniment. The toastmaster calls

---

* Twenty-sixth in the Order of Precedence of London's Livery Companies.

for silence before the Master says to the head chef, 'Chef, as Master of this ancient Company, it is my duty to require of you to pledge that this Roast Beef is fit for consumption by this assembled company, and if so to join me in a mug of English beer. Do you so pledge?' The head chef replies to the Master, 'I am pleased to testify as to the excellence of this beef and gladly join with you in a mug of English beer.' The Master tries a slice of beef and has some beer with the head chef before the beef is carried back to the kitchen.

On 19th July 1821, to celebrate the coronation of King George IV, a Baron of Beef weighing 200 pounds (90 kg) was served to 700 children in the marketplace in Kingston-upon-Thames.

Saint George (c. AD 275/281–23rd April 303) was born in Lydda in Roman Palestine. He was a soldier in the Roman army and was later venerated as a Christian martyr. Saint George is one of the most venerated saints in the Catholic, Anglican, Eastern Orthodox, and the Oriental Orthodox churches. He is immortalised in the story of Saint George and the Dragon and is one of the Fourteen Holy Helpers.

Saint George is regarded as one of the most prominent military saints. Apart from at least 18 countries and 26 cities, he is patron saint of sufferers from leprosy, the plague, herpes and syphilis.

Recipe

(From *The Epicurean*, by Charles Ranhofer)

The baron of beef weighs about a hundred and fifty pounds. It's the saddle of beef cut from the hip of a young and tender ox as far down as the second rib, this being pared and the thinnest part covered with slices of fat so as to have the meat of uniform thickness and cooked alike throughout. It takes about five hours to cook a baron of beef in a baker's brick oven, the best to use for large pieces of this description. After being cooked they should be put in a heater or warm place, for about two hours, to finish cooking slowly. When cooked, arrange it on a large dish, garnishing on the edges with shavings of horseradish and the ends with Yorkshire Pudding. Serve thickened gravy well skimmed and strained through a fine sieve, in a separate sauce-boat, also some baked potatoes.

Beef Steak Leopold I

Steak with pepper and butter.

The recipe comes from George Leonard Herter's book *Bull Cook and Authentic Historical Recipes and Practices*. I discovered the recipe via *The Neglected Books Page* where Brad Bigelow describes

Herter: 'Among the cognoscenti, George Leonard Herter (1911–94) is treasured as one of the great American nutcases of all time, a man who never let nonsense like facts or objective sources tarnish the immaculate lunacy of his notions.'

Quite how Herter came to name his dish after the Belgian king is a mystery. He was, however, well known as a food lover.

Following Belgium's independence from the Netherlands, on 21st July 1831 **Leopold I** (1790–1865) became the first king of the Belgians. He was the founder of the Belgian line of the House of Saxe-Coburg and Gotha and was well liked by the Belgians.

In 1816, he had married Princess Charlotte of Wales, the only legitimate child of the British Prince Regent (later King George IV) and therefore second in line to the British throne. Sadly, on 5th November 1817, Princess Charlotte delivered a stillborn son and she herself died the following day. Had she lived, she would have become Queen of the United Kingdom on the death of her father, and Leopold presumably would have assumed the role later taken by his nephew, Prince Albert of Saxe-Coburg and Gotha, as Prince Consort of the United Kingdom, and never been chosen to reign as King of the Belgians.

Leopold not only had a taste for good food but an eye for beautiful women. His second wife was Louise Marie of Orleans (1812–50), a real beauty and daughter of King Louis Philippe of France. Both Leopold and Louise were expert cooks. Leopold, a great eater, both collected and created recipes.

Recipe

(From *Bull Cook and Authentic Historical Recipes and Practices*, by George Leonard Herter)

Take your beef steak, whatever kind that you desire and lay it onto a plate. Salt it on both sides to taste. Now take your pepper mill and grind a thin coating of pepper over one side of the steak. Take your finger tips and press the pieces of pepper into the meat as much as possible. Turn the steak over and do the same for the other side. Now grill your steak. Remove it when done as you desire it and quickly take a heaping spoonful of butter and spread it over the entire steak. The butter blends with the herb flavours of the pepper and gives the steak the best flavour you have ever tasted in a steak. It does something for beef that you just would not believe possible until you tasted it.

Sirloin of Beef à la Ferdinand de Lesseps

History doesn't relate what exactly **Sirloin of Beef à la Ferdinand de Lesseps** was, but we do know who he was and when the dish was served.

Ferdinand de Lesseps (1805–94) was the French builder of the Suez Canal, and the first to try to build *a* Panama Canal. He was honoured with a dinner at Delmonico's restaurant in New York on Monday, 1st March 1880.

Aperire Terram Gentibus ('To open the world to all people') was de Lesseps' family motto.

Not content with naming a sirloin of beef after de Lesseps that evening, Delmonico also named a banana dessert 'à la Panama'.

Biff à la Lindström

This is named after **Henrik Lindström** (1831–1910), a prominent Swedish industrialist. Though he came from a Swedish family, Lindström was actually born and bred in Saint Petersburg in Russia.

Lindström often ate at the Hotel Witt in Kalmar in south-east Sweden, and it was there that on Sunday, 4th May 1862 the story of **Biff à la Lindström** began.

Lindndström was at the hotel with a group of friends and wanted to introduce them to something special that he used to eat in Russia. He asked for various ingredients to be brought to the table: minced beef, finely chopped red beetroot, potatoes, onions, eggs, capers, salt and pepper. He then mixed and stirred everything together, and from this made beef patties, which were then taken into the kitchen to be fried in butter. The result was a success all round. When the restaurateur asked, 'What shall we call this invention?', the answer was obvious – 'Biff à la Lindström.' Since that day, there has always been a version of Biff à la Lindström on the menu at the Hotel Witt.

Prarie Dog 'Bat' Masterson

William Barclay 'Bat' Masterson (1853–1921) was one of the early law officers at Dodge City, Kansas, and a great friend of Wyatt Earp's. Bat was an excellent gunfighter. He was a short, stubby man with a friendly homespun appearance that made him look like anything but a gunfighter. In later years he became a New York sports writer. He was not a heavy drinker. He preferred lemon pop to alcoholic drinks and drank large quantities of it. His favourite foods were cold tongue sandwiches and wiener sandwiches. Bat created wiener sandwiches which became well known throughout the Old West and was justly thought of as a real delicacy. Everyone called it a **Prairie Dog**. It is one of the greatest wiener recipes ever made and will be remembered long after Bat's gun deeds are forgotten.

Recipe

(From *Bull Cook and Authentic Historical Recipes and Practices*, by George Leonard Herter)

Take a wiener and slit it open lengthwise. Take ground sage and rub plenty of it into the slit and onto the sides of the slit. Put the wiener in an oven and broil until done. Take a bun and on one side of it put mustard and thinly sliced dill pickles. On the other side sprinkle it well with Worcestershire Sauce. The sage, mustard and Worcestershire

Sauce blend together to give you a sandwich with a wonderful taste. Be sure to try this famous sandwich at your first opportunity. It makes the usual catsup and mustard wiener sandwich taste very poor in comparison.

Beef Minion Giacomo Meyerbeer

A beef minion is a steak cut from the smaller end of a tenderloin.

Giacomo Meyerbeer (1791–1864), born Jacob Liebmann Beer, was a German opera composer of Jewish birth who has been described as perhaps the most successful stage composer of the 19th century.

His 1824 opera, *Il crociato in Egitto*, was the first to bring him a Europe-wide reputation, but it was *Robert le diable* (1831) which raised his status to that of great celebrity. His public career from 1831 until his death, during which he remained throughout a dominating figure in the world of opera, was summarised by his contemporary Hector Berlioz, who claimed that he 'has not only the luck to be talented, but the talent to be lucky'. He was at his peak with his operas *Les Huguenots* (1836) and *Le Prophète* (1849). His last opera, *L'Africaine*, was performed posthumously. His works made him the most frequently performed composer at the world's leading opera houses in the 19th century.

Recipe

Carefully trim a tenderloin of beef, remove all the fat and nerves, then cut it into slices, each one weighing five ounces; beat them lightly to have them all of the same thickness, then pare and cut them into round shapes. Salt them on both sides, dip them in melted butter and grill them. They should take six minutes if desired rare, eight minutes to have them properly done, and ten minutes if required well done. Prepare a Piedmontese risotto (with wine, wild mushrooms and truffles). Garnish the centre of a dish with this, piling it high. Glaze the minions, and arrange them around the rice. Divide some lamb or mutton kidneys in two, having half a kidney for each minion; season these with salt and pepper, then sauté them in some hot butter. When they are done, drain off the butter, add a little fresh butter and some meat glaze, and toss the kidneys in this. Lay half a kidney on top of each minion, serving at the same time, a sauce boat of sauce Perigueux.

Tournedos Rachel

Tournedos Rachel (mignon steak garnished with artichoke bottoms and bone marrow) was devised by the American food writer Raymond Sokolov (b.1941). It first appeared in his splendidly entitled book *The Saucier's Apprenctice*, first published in 1976.

See **Salade Rachel**, page 57, **Eggs Rachel**, page 174, **Filets de Sole Rachel**, page 187, **Vegetables Rachel**, page 237, and the **Rachel Sandwich**, page 258.

Tournedos Rossini

This is a French steak dish, purportedly created for **Rossini** by the French master chef Marie-Antoine Carême (or possibly by the chef at the Savoy Hotel, Auguste Escoffier).

The dish comprises a beef tournedos* (*filet mignon*) fried in butter and served on a croûton, This is then topped with a slice of hot fresh whole *foie gras* fried briefly at the last minute. It is then garnished with slices of black truffle and finished with a Madeira *demi-glace* sauce.

Gioacchino Rossini (1792–1868) had written 39 operas by the time he was 40. He then suddenly retired and later settled in a villa outside Paris where he threw dinner parties and philosophised on music and food.

---

* It was said that the name of the dish was due to the fact that the composer's butler was obliged to *tourner le dos* (turn his back) on Rossini's dinner guests so as to hide the secret of the final touches of this recipe.

According to *Grove's Dictionary of Music and Musicians*, 'No composer in the first half of the 19th century enjoyed the measure of prestige, wealth, popular acclaim or artistic influence that belonged to Rossini. His contemporaries recognized him as the greatest Italian composer of his time.'

Salisbury Steak

Minced beef flavoured with onion and seasoning, and then deep-fried or grilled.

Dr James Henry Salisbury, MD (1823–1905), was a 19th century American doctor, and the inventor of the **Salisbury Steak**. He was one of the earliest health food faddists and taught that diet was the main determinant of health. He believed that vegetables and starchy foods produced poisons in the digestive system which were responsible for heart disease, tumours, mental illness and tuberculosis. He believed that human dentition demonstrated that humans were meant to eat meat, and so sought to limit vegetables, fruit, starches, and fats to no more than a third of the diet.

Salisbury served as a doctor during the American Civil War, and became convinced that the diarrhoea suffered by the troops could be controlled with a diet of coffee and lean chopped beefsteak.

He was an early American proponent of a low-carbohydrate diet for weight loss.

The Salisbury Steak, essentially a hamburger, might have faded from the collective memory if World War I had not inspired a drive in English-speaking countries to rename German sounding things. The British royal family changed its German-sounding name Saxe-Coburg-Gotha to Windsor, and Salisbury Steak became a popular substitute for the Hamburger.

Beef Stroganoff

Strips of beef served with a variety of sauces and known worldwide.

There are two candidates for the Russian aristocrat after whom **Beef Stroganoff** is named:

Count Grigory Dmitriyevich (1656–1715), a Russian landowner and statesman, the most notable member of the prominent Stroganov family in the late 17th and early 18th centuries, and a strong supporter of the reforms and initiatives of Peter the Great. Beginning in 1682 he regularly assisted the government in its financial difficulties. In 1700, Stroganov funded the construction of several military ships for the nascent Imperial Russian Navy.

Count Pavel Alexandrovich Stroganov (1774–1817), a Russian military commander and statesman, lieutenant general, Adjutant General to Alexander I of Russia. He took part in the Privy Committee that outlined the tsar's govenment reform. He commanded an infantry division in the Napoleonic Wars.

It seems that the counts' names always end with a 'v', the beef's mostly with a double 'f'.

Recipe

Elena Molokhovets' classic Russian cookbook *A Gift to Young Housewives* (1861) gives the first known recipe for 'Beef à la Stroganov, with mustard' which involves lightly floured beef *cubes* (not strips) sautéed, sauced with prepared mustard and bouillon, and finished with a small amount of sour cream: no onions, no mushrooms. A competition purported to have taken place in 1890 is sometimes mentioned in the dish's history, but both the recipe and the name existed before then. Another recipe, this one from 1912, adds onions and tomato paste, and serves it with crisp potato straws, which are considered the traditional side dish in Russia. The version given in the 1938 *Larousse Gastronomique* includes beef *strips*, and onions, with either mustard or tomato paste optional.

After the fall of Imperial Russia, the recipe was popularly served in the hotels and restaurants of China before the start of the Second World War. Russian and Chinese immigrants, as well as US servicemen stationed in pre-Communist China, took several variants of the dish to the United States, which may account for its popularity there during the 1950s. It went to Hong Kong in the late fifties, with Russian restaurants and hotels serving the dish with rice, but not sour cream. The version often prepared in restaurants and hotels in the USA today consists of strips of beef fillet with a mushroom, onion, and sour cream sauce. It's served with rice or pasta.

Beef Tegetthoff

There are two rather different sorts of **Beef Tegetthoff**.

Beef Carpaccio Tegetthoff with a rocket salad and parmesan, along with an olive oil balsamic dressing. The second variant is beef served with a seafood ragout.

Admiral Wilhelm von Tegetthoff (1827–71) was an Austrian admiral, considered to be one of the most prominent naval commanders of the 19th century. Tegetthoff was known for his innovative tactics as well as for his inspirational leadership.

Beef Hash Sam Ward

Minced beef with potatoes and corned beef.

Samuel Cutler 'Sam' Ward (1814–84) was a poet, author, lobbyist and gourmet. In the years after the American Civil War he combined delicious food, fine wines, and good conversation to create a new type of lobbying in Washington, DC – 'social lobbying' – over which he reigned for more than a decade; indeed, he was widely known as 'the King of the Lobby.'

Sam's book of poetry, *Lyrical Recreations*, soon sank into obscurity; however his hilarious anonymous magazine accounts of his time in the gold fields were edited into *Sam Ward in the Gold Rush*, published in 1949.

For years after his death, bar patrons ordered 'Sam Wards', a drink he invented of cracked ice, a peel of lemon, and yellow Chartreuse. Restaurants carried Chicken Sauté Sam Ward on their menus for decades. For years Locke-Ober in Boston served a dish called Mushrooms Sam Ward.

He was immortalised by his nephew, the author Francis Marion Crawford, as the delightful Mr Bellingham in his novel *Doctor Claudius*.

Recipe

In a large frying-pan put one ounce of butter; when this is hot add four ounces of potatoes, and six ounces of corned beef, both cut in three-sixteenths of an inch squares. Season with pepper and nutmeg, and fry, slowly inclining the pan so that the hash assumes the shape of an omelette. When it all has a fine colour drain off the butter, and turn the hash on to a long dish the same as an omelette.

Beef Wellington

'Next to a battle lost, the greatest misery is a battle gained.'

A dish of beef, slathered with a mushroom and/or *foie gras* mixture, given a kick by Madeira and baked in pastry.

The name is assumed to be a homage to the great Irish general of the British Army and later Prime Minister, **Arthur Wellesley, 1st Duke of Wellington** (1769–1852), hero of the Battle of Waterloo, whose London abode, Apsley House, is often referred to as 'Number One London'.

Possible origins which have been suggested for the name include:

- Wellington the soldier had no concern at all for what food he was served and so allowed his cook to indulge his own fancies, of which this is one.

- Wellington loved this dish so much it had to be served at every dinner.

- The name arose because its shape resembles the Wellington boot.

- The dish is of central African origin, traditionally using goat meat, and was discovered by Wellington when he served there (which he never did).

- The dish is actually French, but re-named during the 19th-century wars with France.

But **Beef Wellington** doesn't appear in any English cookery book we can find before about 1970, and we can't find it mentioned in literature before Michael Bond's *Paddington Takes the Test* of 1981. It has no known connection, other than the name, with the Duke of Wellington or with the towns of Wellington in Cumbria, Herefordshire, Shropshire, Somerset, or New Zealand. In fact this dish, so often seen as thoroughly English and completely Victorian, appears to be modern, originally French and named in America after an Irishman.

VEAL

Veal Pie à la Dickens

'If there were no bad people, there would be no good lawyers.'

It was almost certainly in 1867, when **Charles Dickens** (1812–70) was making his second visit to North America, that Charles Ranhofer created this dish in his honour at Delmonico's in New York. Ranhofer also had **Beet Fritters à la Dickens** (see page 232) on the menu. Dickens had first visited America from January to June 1842, between the writing of *Barnaby Rudge* and *Martin Chuzzlewit*. His book *Notes on America* was published in October 1842.

Schnitzel à la Holstein

Schnitzel à la Holstein is a German dish that is said to be named after the German diplomat **Friedrich von Holstein** (1837–1909), who liked to be served different kinds of food all on one plate.

Holstein was a statesman of the German Empire. He served as the head of the political department of the German Foreign Office for more than 30 years, and played a major role in shaping foreign policy after Bismarck was dismissed in 1890.

The word *Schnitzel*, in German, mean 'little slice'.

Recipe

The original recipe listed the following: veal cutlet, fried eggs, anchovy, caviar, smoked salmon and mushrooms.

Today's version of the dish has been substantially simplified to veal, egg, capers and anchovy.

Lord Nelson Veal

(Selle de veau à la Nelson)

A braised saddle of veal with ham slices inserted, coated with cheese and truffle purée, baked.

Horatio Nelson, 1st Viscount Nelson (1758–1805) was Britain's greatest naval commander, famous for his inspirational leadership, superb grasp of strategy and unconventional tactics, which resulted in a number of decisive naval victories. These include the Battle of the Nile in 1798, and Britain's greatest naval victory, when Nelson was killed, the Battle of Trafalgar in 1805. Nelson is also remembered for losing the sight of his right eye in Corsica in 1794, and his right arm at the Battle of Santa Cruz de Tenerife in 1797.

His officers and crews were consistently extremely fond of him. The word 'love' crops up again and again in correspondence; most unusual with commanders.

He is also famous for his affair with Lady Hamilton and his last words about which there is still heated debate. Take your pick: 'Thank God, I have done my duty', 'Kiss me, Hardy', 'I have then lived long enough', or 'Do you anchor, Hardy'.

This last was not a question but an order.

See **Spring Lamb Cutlets Nelson**, page 118, and **Lord Nelson Sole**, page 183.

Recipe

(From *Guide to the Art of Modern Cookery* by Auguste Escoffier)

Braise the saddle. When it is ready, remove the fillets... In the cavities left by the fillets spread a few tablespoons full of Soubise; return the colloped fillets to their place, and, between the collops, place a thin slice of ham, of the same size and shape as the adjacent piece of meat, and a little Soubise sauce. Having reconstructed the joint, cover its surface with a layer, about one inch thick, of Soufflé au parmesan, combined with one quart of truffle purée. Bind the joint with a strong band of buttered paper, for the purpose of holding in the soufflé, and set it to cook in a moderate oven for fifteen minutes. After having taken the saddle out of the oven, remove the paper band, and send it to the table without changing the dish. Send the braising-liquor, cleared of all grease, reduced and strained, to the table separately.

Veal à la Prince Orloff

Veal à la Prince Orloff is a 19th-century Russian dish. It consists of a braised loin of veal, thinly sliced, with a thin layer of puréed mushrooms and onions between each slice, and topped with a **Mornay Sauce** (see page 225) and browned in the oven.

While we are sure about what goes into the dish we aren't so sure about who it honoured. There are four possible candidates:

The first was **Prince Grigoryevich Orlov** (1734–83), a one-time lover of Catherine the Great. The dish was purportedly created by the prince's unnamed French chef.

The next possibility is that it was created for **Prince Alexey Fyodorovich Orlov** (1787–1862), nephew of the above, or else Alexey's brother

Mikhail Fyodorovich Orlov (1788–1842). Some food historians suggest that the dish was invented by Marie-Antoine Carême, whose dates would imply that it was indeed for one of the two brothers.

Finally there is Alexey's son **Prince Nikolay Alexeyevich Orlov** (1827–85), a distinguished Russian diplomat and author. He first adopted a military career, and was seriously wounded in the Crimean War. Subsequently he entered the diplomatic service, and represented Russia successively at Brussels, Paris and Berlin. His articles on corporal punishment, which appeared in *Russkaya Starina* in 1881, brought about its abolition. In the early 1860s his wife Katherine (Kathi) had a close relationship with Otto von Bismarck. Bismarck's wife Johanna was reportedly not jealous and credited Kathi with a long period of Bismarck's happiness.

It has been said that whichever prince it was, it was probably one who disliked veal, and the sauces were to mask the exact nature of meat. Also the sauces might well have been used to mask the smell of not very fresh veal.

Veal Oscar

Veal cutlets medallions with asparagus, and lobster or crab meat, topped with Béarnaise Sauce.

Veal Oscar was named for **Oscar II** (1829–1907), King of Sweden from

1872 until his death, and King of Norway from 1872 until Norway's independence in 1905.

Oscar was a writer, poet, amateur musician, mathematician and theatre lover. He commissioned a new opera house for the Royal Swedish Opera. It is still their home today. Oscar once told Henrik Ibsen that his *Ghosts* was 'not a good play'.

As he was dying, the king asked for the theatres not be closed on account of his death. His wishes were respected.

Veal Cutlets Pojarski

(Kotiety pojarskie)

The story is that these were originally made with beef and were a favourite of Tsar Nicholas I (1796–1855). One day the tsar arrived at an inn and the owner, **Pojarski**, hastily prepared the dish with veal instead of beef. This greatly pleased Nicholas.

Recipe

The recipe calls for the meat to be removed from a veal chop, then minced and blended with butter, seasonings and bread soaked in milk. The chop is then reformed and sautéed in clarified butter.

Wallenberg Steaks

Veal hamburger steaks usually served with potato purée, boiled green peas and lingonberry jam or lingonberries sweetened with sugar.

This classic Swedish dish takes its name from the distinguished Swedish family of financiers, the **Wallenbergs**. It seems most likely that the dish got its name when Marcus Wallenberg (1864–1943) married chef Charles Emil Hagdahl's daughter Amalia. A similar recipe is to be found in Hagdahl's cookery book *Kokkonsten*, which Amalia helped him write. The book includes more than 3,000 recipes.

Recipe

(Adapted from a recipe on Swedish radio programme '*Söndag, Söndag*')

- 400 g of minced veal (or beef)
- 4 egg yolks
- 200 ml of double cream
- 4 ml of salt
- A dash of four-spice powder [see below] or white pepper
- Fresh breadcrumbs
- Clarified butter

Four Spice Powder

- 1 tablespoon of ground white pepper
- 1 teaspoon of ground ginger
- 1 teaspoon of grated nutmeg
- ¼ of a teaspoon of ground cloves

Mix the minced veal, the egg yolks, the cream and the spices in a food processor or a blender – the mixture must be very smooth. Form the mixture into four hamburger steaks. Don't make them too thick.

Coat the steaks in fresh breadcrumbs and fry them in clarified butter on both sides until browned and done.

LAMB

Lamb Chops Victor Hugo

'Music expresses that which cannot be said and on which it is impossible to be silent.'

Lamb chops with horseradish, garlic and parmesan.

Victor Marie Hugo (1802–85) was a French Romantic poet, novelist, and dramatist. He is considered one of the greatest French writers and is perhaps best known for *Les Misérables* and *The Hunchback of Notre Dame*.

Recipe

For two

- 4 lamb chops
- 1 clove of garlic, peeled and halved
- 2 tablespoons of oil
- 3 teaspoons of horseradish sauce
- 1 cup of thick white sauce
- ¼ of a cup of fresh white breadcrumbs

¼ of a cup of grated parmesan cheese

Rub the chops with the garlic and then brown them on both sides in the hot oil. Drain them and put them into a buttered ovenproof dish. Stir the horseradish into the white sauce together and spoon it over the chops. Mix the breadcrumbs and cheese together, then sprinkle them over the sauce. Cover and bake at 200°C for half an hour. Remove the cover and continue cooking for a further 15 minutes.

Lamb Cutlets Bartolomé Esteban Murillo

(Côtelettes d'agneau à la Murillo)

Bartolomé Esteban Murillo (1617–82) was a Spanish Baroque painter. Murillo was the leading painter in Seville in the later 17th century. He remained one of the most admired and popular of all European artists in the 18th and early 19th centuries. There are at least seven of his pictures in the National Gallery in London. These include a fine self portrait.

Recipe

(From *The Epicurean*, by Charles Ranhofer)

Pare twelve lamb cutlets having them both wide and thin; range them in a *sautoir* with hot butter, laying them all one way; cook on one side only, then drain and cover this cooked side with slightly cold minced mushrooms, reduced and thickened with some good béchamel, finishing with a dash of cayenne pepper. Smooth the surface of these mushrooms nicely, dredge over with grated parmesan and sprinkle with melted butter. Return the chops to the *sautoir* and set it in the hot oven to finish cooking and brown. Dress them at once on separate plates with a little halt-glaze on the bottom and hand them to the guests.

Spring Lamb Cutlets Nelson

(Côtelettes d'agneau de lait Nelson)

Lamb cutlets with croûtons, asparagus and *foie gras*.

Named for **Lord Nelson** (1758–1805), the hero of the Battle of Trafalgar, 21st October 1805.

The 21st October used to be, and I believe still should be, celebrated as Trafalgar Day. It is still respected in the Royal Navy where on Trafalgar Night grand dinners are held with each dish being given a fanciful Nelsonian name such as 'Victory Desert', and a toast made to 'the immortal memory of Lord Nelson and those who fell with him'.

See **Lord Nelson Veal**, page 108, and **Lord Nelson Sole**, page 183.

Having once said 'Treat every Frenchman as if he was the devil himself', I'm quite sure that Nelson wouldn't have approved of a recipe by Escoffier. Nevertheless:

Recipe

(From *A Guide to the Art of Modern Cookery*, by Auguste Escoffier)

Grill the cutlets, and, at the same time, prepare as many breadcrumb croûtons as there are cutlets, and of exactly the same shape as the latter. Fry the croûtons in butter, and coat them with *foie gras* purée.

Put a slice of truffle on the centre of each cutlet, and each cutlet on a croûton and sprinkle over the parmesan. Arrange the cutlets in a circle and put them in the oven for five minutes.

After taking them out of the oven, garnish the centre of the dish with a heap of asparagus-heads, covered with butter.

Hind Saddle of Lamb à la Paganini

(Selle d'agneau à la Paganini)

Niccolò Paganini (1782–1840) owned a number of very fine string instruments. While he was still a teenager in Livorno, a wealthy businessman named Livron lent him a violin for a concert. The violin was made by the master luthier Giuseppe Guarneri. Livron was so impressed with Paganini's playing that he refused to take the violin back. This particular violin came to be known as *Il Cannone Guarnerius*. On a later occasion in Parma, Paganini won another valuable violin (also by Guarneri) after a difficult sight-reading challenge from a man named Pasini.

The *Caprice no. 24 in A minor* is probably Paganini's best known composition.

Recipe

(From *The Epicurean*, by Charles Ranhofer)

Have the saddle prepared and cooked the same as for Florentine [see below]; dress the meat and garnish around with slices of *foie gras* intercalated with slices of truffles; cover these with a supreme sauce and lay on top partridge quenelles decorated with truffles. The saddle may be garnished with skewers thrust into it composed of double cocks'-combs and glazed truffles. Serve a sauce-bowl of supreme sauce at the same time as the saddle.

Hind Saddle Of Lamb à la Florentine

Roast a saddle of yearling lamb in the oven having it laid in a baking pan; salt and baste with dripping. It will take from an hour to an hour and a half to have it properly roasted if the oven be very hot. When done, dress and glaze the meat, surround it with a garnishing of artichoke bottoms à la Florence, and serve with a separate white Colbert Sauce.

PORK

∾

Dongpo Pork

Chinese belly of pork with ginger and spring onions.

Su Dongpo (1037–1101), also known as Su Shi (not to be confused with Sushi) was a Chinese writer, poet, painter, calligrapher, pharmacologist, gastronome, and statesman.

Recipe

(From www.allrecipes.com)

For six.

- 1 lb of raw pork belly
- 3 tablespoons of vegetable oil
- ¼ cup of light soy sauce
- ¼ cup of dark soy sauce
- ½ cup of Chinese rice cooking wine
- 3½ oz of Chinese rock sugar
- 1 in piece of fresh ginger, peeled and grated
- 8 spring onions, sliced

Slice the pork belly into 2-inch wide strips. Bring a large pot of water to a boil, and stir in the pork slices. Reduce heat to a simmer, and cook the meat for 10 minutes. Remove it from the water, and blot it dry with paper towels.

Heat the vegetable oil over medium high heat in a large wok, and brown the pork strips well on all sides. The pork will splatter.

While the pork is browning, mix together the light soy sauce, dark soy sauce, rice wine, rock sugar, ginger, and spring onions in a large pot. Bring the mixture to a boil, stirring to dissolve the sugar. Reduce heat to a gentle simmer, and put the pork strips into the liquid. Cover, and simmer until the meat is very tender, 1½ to 2 hours. Add water as needed to keep the liquid from going completely dry.

Chinese rock sugar is available at specialty and Asian grocery stores. If you can't find it, use brown sugar.

A dash of five-spice powder is delicious.

GAME

~

Oreiller de la Belle Aurore

This is a large, square, raised pie dedicated to Jean-Anthèlme Brillat-Savarin's mother, **Claudine Aurore Récamier**, known as '*La Belle Aurore*'.

The large, square pie, which was one of her son's favourite meals, contains a variety of game birds and their livers, veal, pork, truffles, aspic, and more, all in puff pastry. It is described in the classic encyclopaedia of gastronomy, *Larousse Gastronomique*. It is one of three pies named after people from Brillat-Savarin's home town of Belley (later called Bugey). They were described by Lucien Tenret. The others were *Chapeau de Monseigneur Cortois de Quinsey* and *Toque du Président Adolphe Clerc*.

An **Oreiller de la Belle Aurore** is said to have caused the death of Anthèlme Brillat-Savarin's violin teacher, who one day just ate far too much of it.

Rissoles à la Demidoff

Pheasant rissoles with mushrooms and truffles.

Count Anatoly Nikolaievich Demidov (called Anatole), 1st Prince of San Donato (1813–70), was a Russian industrialist, diplomat and patron of the arts.

He was born in Saint Petersburg or Moscow, but grew up in Paris, where his father was ambassador. He served briefly as a diplomat himself in Paris, Rome and Venice. On his father's death in 1828, Anatole settled for good in Western Europe, returning to Russia as little as possible. This attitude alienated him from Tsar Nicholas I, who had always had an antipathy towards him.

Both Demidov and his mother, Elisabeth Stroganova, were extreme admirers of Napoleon, to the point where Demidov had a brief marriage to Napoleon's niece Princess Mathilde; he also bought the Elba house of exile to turn into a museum. He was famous as a patron of artists, and a *bon vivant*.

He considerably expanded the Demidov collection assembled by his father at the Villa San Donato near Florence. In 1834 he acquired Paul Delaroche's *The Execution of Lady Jane Grey* (now in the

National Gallery in London). He commissioned paintings from Eugène Delacroix, Richard Parkes Bonington and Théodore Géricault. The collection was split up in 1863, seven years before the prince's death in 1870.

In 1839 the writer Jules Janin introduced him into the circle of the former king of Westphalia, Jérôme Bonaparte, who was living in exile in Florence. A plan to marry Jérôme's daughter, Princess Mathilde-Létizia Bonaparte, to Demidov was quickly formed.

In 1840, in order to allow the princess to hold onto her title, a decree made Demidov 'prince of San Donato', though the title was never recognised in Russia. The marriage took place on 1st November 1840, but sadly the relationship soon soured, with the princess taking Count Émilien de Nieuwerkerke as a lover, and Demidov taking Valentine de Sainte-Aldegonde, duchesse de Dino, as a mistress.

One evening, during a ball, Mathilde made a violent scene with Valentine, with the result that Demidov slapped her twice in public. The couple soon separated.

Demidov tried to repair the damage the separation did to his social standing by increasing his charitable donations. He founded hospitals and orphanages and started an international committee to help prisoners of the Crimean War.

Demidov was known to be 'one of the greatest gastronomes of the Second Empire'.

See **Chicken Demidoff**, page 144, and **Red Snapper à la Demidoff**, page 176.

Recipe

Roll out some brioche paste to one-eighth of an inch in thickness; divide it into rounds with a channelled three and a half inch in diameter pastry cutter, and lay in the centre of each a ball of preparation an inch and a half in diameter. Wet around these, fold over, and fasten the two edges together, then lay them on a floured cloth, and leave them to rise in a mild temperature until double their height; fry them slowly in very hot fat so that the paste be thoroughly cooked and serve when done on folded napkins. For the preparation cut about two ounces of mushrooms, two ounces of truffles and two ounces of breast of pheasant; heat well with *velouté* sauce until boiling point; allow to cool; use this preparation to garnish the rissoles.

Game Saint Hubert of Liège

Saint Hubert of Liège (656–727) is the patron saint of Belgium as well as the hunt and of everything associated with it.

Legend has it that Hubert was a wealthy, pleasure-loving, young Belgian aristocrat, and of all the possible pleasures of the rich and self-indulgent, he loved hunting the most. One Good Friday, the stag he was pursuing in the forest turned toward him and Hubert saw that there was a crucifix between his antlers. Hubert not only saw a crucifix, he saw the error of his worldly ways, promptly relinquished them, and became a bishop.

Saint Hubert's Day (3rd November) is the beginning of the hunting season in many parts of Europe. In many places it is celebrated with a stag hunt, which seems an awfully odd way to celebrate the life of a man who gave up hunting for religious reasons.

The traditional Saint Hubert's Day hunt begins with the blessing of special bread, which is then shared out amongst the hunting dogs in the belief that it will protect them from rabies. Other than the bread, all dishes 'à la St Hubert' are based on some sort of game. There is a good selection: consommé, purée of pheasant (or any game), tournedos of venison, *petites bouchées* (or *vol-au-vents*), *timbales*, and even an omelette.

See **Omelette Saint Hubert**, page 169.

Wild Duck à la Walter Scott

'O, what a tangled web we weave when first we practise to deceive!'

Sir Walter Scott, 1st Baronet (1771–1832) was a Scottish historical novelist, playwright, and poet. He was the first English-language author to have a truly international career in his lifetime, with many contemporary readers in Europe, Australia, and North America. His most famous novels include *Ivanhoe, Rob Roy, The Lady of the Lake, Waverley, The Heart of Midlothian* and *The Bride of Lammermoor*.

Throughout his career Scott combined his writing with his daily occupation as Clerk of Session and Sheriff-Depute of Selkirkshire. He was a prominent member of the Tory establishment in Edinburgh and an active member of the Highland Society. From 1820–23 he served as President of the Royal Society of Edinburgh.

Recipe

(From the *Larousse Gastronomique*)

Draw, singe and truss a wild duck. Cook in a pre-heated oven at 200°C, 425°F, Gas Mark 7. Meanwhile, fry the duck's liver in butter, mash and mix it with 20 g (¾ oz) of foie gras. Fry 2 croûtons in clarified butter and spread them with the liver paste. Core 2 apples, stud each with 4 cloves and cook as for Apples Bonne Femme [see below]. Dilute some Dundee marmalade with 2 tablespoons of whisky and heat gently. When the duck is cooked, arrange it on a serving dish. Remove the cloves from the apples and put the latter on the croûtons, then pour the marmalade into the holes in the apples. Arrange the croûtons around the duck. Serve the juice in a gravy boat, without skimming off the fat.

Apples Bonne Femme

Make a light, circular incision round the middle of some firm cooking apples. Core them and then put them in a large, buttered ovenproof dish. Fill the hollow in each apple with butter mixed with caster sugar. Pour a few tablespoons of water into the dish. Cook in the oven at 220°C, 425°F, Gas Mark 7 until the apples are tender.

Woodcock Salmis Agnès Sorel

Woodcock garnished with button mushrooms, breast of chicken and pickled ox tongue.

Agnès Sorel (1422–50) was a favourite mistress of King Charles VII of France, by whom she had three daughters. She is considered the first officially recognised royal mistress, and was known as *Dame de Beauté*, not because of her undoubted beauty, but after the château at Beauté-sur-Marne which Charles gave her. She was known as *La reine sans couronne* ('The queen without a crown').

Agnès Sorel is said to have had a great interest in food and its preparation. Her name has been given to a soup, a garnish, to timbales and tartlets. In particular she is remembered for **Woodcock Salmis Agnès Sorel**, the dish she is said to have created herself.

Squabs à la Umberto

Umberto I (1844–1900), Umberto Ranieri Carlo Emanuele Giovanni Maria Ferdinando Eugenio di Savoia was king of Italy from 1878 until his death. He was nicknamed *il Buono* (the Good).

Umberto's reign saw Italy attempt colonial expansion into the Horn of Africa, successfully gaining Eritrea and Somalia, despite being defeated in 1896 by Abyssinia at the Battle of Adowa. In 1882, he approved the Triple Alliance with the German Empire and Austria-Hungary.

Umberto was loathed in leftist circles and especially hated by anarchists, who attempted to assassinate him during the first year of his reign.

On 28th July 1900, Umberto went to a small restaurant in Monza for dinner, accompanied by his aide-de-camp, General Emilio Ponzia-Vaglia. When the restaurant's owner came out to take the king's order personally, Umberto was surprised that he and the owner were virtual doubles, both in face and in build. They began discussing their striking resemblance to one another and found many more similarities:

- Both men shared the same name, Umberto.

- Both men were born on the same day, in the same year, March 14th, 1844.

- Both were born in the same town.

- Both married a woman called Margherita.

- Both were married on the same day.

- Both had a son called Vittorio.

- Both had served in the Italian Army, albeit in different ranks.

- King Umberto was crowned on the same day that the other Umberto opened his restaurant.

The king was so impressed by all these coincidences that he invited the other Umberto to visit the royal palace the following day. Sadly Umberto the restaurateur couldn't take up the invitation, as he had died in a shooting accident. The final coincidence was that King Umberto died that same day, shot through the heart by an anarchist, Gaetano Bresci.

Recipe

Butter or oil as many oval paper cases as there are squabs to be prepared; put them in the oven to stiffen and brown, then drain. Bone the birds, stuff them with a delicate quenelle forcemeat into which mix chopped truffles and mushrooms; lay them in a *sautoir* in oval rings of the same diameter as the cases, moisten with a little *mirepoix* stock, reduce it to a glaze, then remoisten to half the height of the squabs, and when done the stock ought to be well reduced; lay them in the cases and cover over with African sauce, dress and serve.

CHICKEN

Poularde Albufera

Poularde Albufera is an elaborate dish where chicken is poached with a garnish of *vol-au-vents* filled with quenelles, cocks' kidneys, mushrooms and truffles in an Albufera Sauce.

Escoffier gives a recipe for this sauce in *Le Guide culinaire*. It consists of a base of Suprême Sauce to which is added a meat glaze, which gives it its characteristic ivory-white tint.

It was named in honour of **Louis Gabriel Suchet, 1st Duke of Albufera** (1770–1826). Suchet was a Marshal of France and one of Napoleon's most brilliant generals.

The recipe is sometimes credited to the French chef Adolphe Dugléré. However, as Dugléré was only ten years old when, in 1815, Albufera fell out of favour with King Louis XVIII, and had his French title taken away, it's much more likely that Poularde Albufera was created by the great chef who had trained Dugléré, Antoine Carême.

Chicken Cardinal la Balue

A dish of chicken pieces sautéed, then roast, and served with crayfish tails and crayfish butter.

Jean Balue (c.1421–91) was a French cardinal and minister of Louis XI. In 1461 he became vicar-general of the bishop of Angers. His cunning and mastery of intrigue gained him the appreciation of Louis XI, who made him his almoner. In 1465 he received the bishopric of Evreux. The king then made him *le premier du grand conseil*, and, in spite of his dissolute life, in 1468 obtained for him a cardinalate. However, in that year Balue was compromised in the king's humiliation by Charles the Bold at Péronne and excluded from the council. He then intrigued with Charles against his master; their secret correspondence was intercepted, and on 23rd April 1469 Balue was thrown into prison, where he remained for 11 years – though not, as has been alleged, in an iron cage. In 1480, through the intervention of Pope Sixtus IV, Balue was freed, and from then on lived in high favour at the court of Rome. In 1484 he was even sent as papal legate to France.

Chicken Fillets Sadi Carnot

Chicken breasts with shallot, truffles, mushrooms, egg yolks and a tomato and Béarnaise Sauce.

Marie François Sadi Carnot (1837–94), was the 4th President of the 3rd French Republic.

While it is possible that this dish was named for the father of thermodynamics, it is far more likely that the chef Charles Ranhofer had Marie François Sadi Carnot in mind and not the president's uncle, physicist **Nicolas Léonard Sadi Carnot** (1796–1832).

The nephew was named after the uncle, who in turn was named after the medieval Persian poet Sa'di (Saadi).

The younger Sadi Carnot was a civil engineer, politician, and government minister who rose to become a popular French president (1887–94), noted for his integrity. He was, however, assassinated by an Italian anarchist, Sante Geronimo Caserio, on 25th June 1894. Caserio was guillotined on 14th August that year.

CHICKEN

Recipe

To be made with twelve chicken breasts. Fry a chopped shallot in butter, keeping it quite colourless and add to it two tablespoonsful of finely minced truffles, three tablespoonsful of finely chopped fresh mushrooms and a teaspoonful of chopped parsley; fry the whole for a few moments on the fire, then add a little chicken glaze, season and let get partially cold before stirring in three raw egg-yolks. Remove the skin and epidermis from the breasts and cut five gashes on the top of the minion fillets; introduce in each gash a thin round of truffle half an inch in diameter form the fillets into rings and lay them in a buttered *sautoir*, filling their interiors with quenelle forcemeat and on top of this set a five-eighths of an inch round of truffle. Split the large fillets through their sides and fill them with the above preparation, then range them in a *sautoir* with clarified butter and lemon juice; sauté, drain, garnish with favor frills and dress in a circle on half heart-shaped croûtons of breadcrumbs fried in butter, cover with a tomato sauce and Béarnaise Sauce, mixed and garnish around the large fillets with the minion fillets, glazing the slices of truffles with meat glaze.

Chicken Demidoff

This is an elaborate chicken dish consisting of chicken sautéed in butter, served with puréed root vegetables, artichoke hearts and onion rings, and topped with a slice of truffle. The cooking juices are then mixed with Madeira and *demi-glace*.

See **Rissoles à la Demidoff**, page 129, and **Red Snapper à la Demidoff**, page 176.

Poularde Edouarde VII

A dish of chicken stuffed with rice, poached, and served with a curry sauce.

To quote *The Foods of England*, **Edward VII** (1841–1910) was 'a sufficiently enthusiastic gourmand to achieve a double heart attack and to have several dishes named after him.'

This one originated at the Carlton Hotel in London on the occasion of his coronation on Saturday, 9th August 1902. The event had originally been scheduled for 26th June of that year, but the ceremony had to be postponed at very short notice as the king was taken ill with an abdominal abscess that required immediate surgery.

See **Coburg Soup**, page 26.

Recipe

(From *A Guide to the Art of Modern Cookery*, by Auguste Escoffier)

Stuff the pullet with rice and poach it without colouration. Dish it, and coat it with a curry sauce, combined with two ounces of diced red pepper per pint of sauce.

Serve a garnish of cucumbers with cream, separately.

Chicken à la King

A dish of diced chicken, mushrooms, green peppers, and pimientos in a cream sherry sauce served on toast.

There are several competing accounts about the origin of this dish:

One claims it was created by the chef at Delmonico's in New York,

Charles Ranhofer, as 'Chicken à la Keene' in the 1880s or 90s, and named after a **Mr or a Mrs Foxhall Parker Keene**.

A second version says it was created in 1881 at Claridge's Hotel in London and named after the sportsman **James R. Keene**, the father of Foxhall Parker Keene. This was to celebrate the fact that JRK's horse (possibly also named Foxall!) had just won the *Grand Prix* in Paris.

Still at Claridge's is the version which says the chef there named it after his father, **J.R. King**.

A fourth account has it that the chef George Greenwald of the Brighton Beach Hotel in Brighton Beach, New York, created it in 1898 (or possibly in the early 1900s) for the owners of the hotel **Mr and Mrs E. Clarke King II**. The following day, either because Mr King had loved it and wanted it on the menu, or because Greenwald asked if he could put it on the menu, that was where it appeared, at $1.25. It quickly became a great success.

Yet another and very plausible account however, is that Chicken à la King was devised in the 1890s by the hotel cook **William 'Bill' King** of the Bellevue Hotel in Philadelphia. After he died on 4th March 1915, several obituaries credited him. A *New York Tribune* editorial at the time said:

'The name of William King is not listed among the great ones of the earth. No monuments will ever be erected to his memory, for he was only a cook. Yet what a cook! In him blazed the fire of genius which, at the white heat of inspiration, drove him one day, in the old Bellevue, in Philadelphia, to combine bits of chicken, mushrooms, truffles, red and green peppers and cream in that delight-some mixture which ever after has been known as *Chicken à la King*.'

It should be noted that the recipe was actually mentioned in the *New York Times* in 1893, and *The Fannie Farmer Cookbook* included a recipe for Chicken à la King in its 1906 update.

It became a popular dish during the middle to late 20th century.

Kung Pao Chicken

Kung Pao Chicken, also known as 'Gong Bao' or 'Kung Po', is a spicy stirfry dish made with chicken, peanuts, vegetables, and chili peppers. This classic dish in Sichuan cuisine originated in the Sichuan Province of south-western China and includes Sichuan peppercorns. The dish is found throughout China, though there are regional variations that are typically less spicy than the Sichuan version. It has also become a staple of westernised Chinese cuisine.

The dish is believed to be named after **Ding Baozhen** (1820–86), a late Qing Dynasty official, and governor of Sichuan Province. His title was *Gongbao* (or *Kung-pao*), literally 'Palace Guardian'. The name 'Kung Pao Chicken' is derived from the title.

During the Cultural Revolution (1966–76), the dish's name became politically incorrect because of its association with Ding and so was renamed 'Hongbao Jiding' (fast-fried chicken cubes) or 'Hula Jiding' (chicken cubes with seared chilies) until its political rehabilitation in the 1980s.

Chaudfroid of Chicken à la Clara Morris

Clara Morris, original name Clara Morrison (1849–1925), was an American actress and writer, known chiefly for her realistic portrayals of unfortunate women in melodrama.

Morris was the eldest child of a bigamous marriage. When she was three, her father was exposed, and her mother fled with her to Cleveland, Ohio, where they adopted her grandmother's name, Morrison. Clara received very little schooling, and in about 1860 became a dancer in the resident ballet company of the Cleveland Academy of Music. She shortened her name to Morris.

In September 1870 Morris made her New York début as Anne Sylvester in Wilkie Collins' *Man and Wife*. The role had come to her by chance, but Morris made such an impression that over the next three years she was featured in a series of highly emotional roles.

Clara Morris also toured extensively, especially in the 1880s. Although neither a great beauty nor a great artist, she had an instinctive genius for portraying the impassioned and often suffering heroines of French melodrama. The passing of the vogue for that sort of theatre, together with her uncertain health, brought her career to a close in the 1890s.

In retirement in New York, Morris contributed articles on acting to various magazines, wrote a daily newspaper column for ten years, and published several books, including *Life on the Stage: My Personal Experiences and Recollections*, published in 1901, and *The Life of a Star*, published in 1906.

Recipe

(From *The Epicurean*, by Charles Ranhofer)

Raise the fillets from six medium two-pound chickens; remove the skin and cuticle, pare them carefully into half-hearts; salt over and lay them in a buttered *sautoir* in such a way that all the pointed ends are in the centre; cover with clarified butter and squeeze over the juice of a lemon; put them on the fire to fry without colouring, then drain and put them under a weight to press lightly; pare them again so that they are all the same shape. Bone the second joints, keeping on half of the drumstick bones, remove the sinews and season the meats with salt, pepper and nutmeg; stuff the inside with a quenelle forcemeat , into which mix a quarter as much *foie gras* rubbed through a sieve and the same quantity of truffles, tongue and pistachios cut in three-sixteenths inch squares. Enclose the dressing well and sew the skin together to envelop it completely, then put these legs in a *sautoir* covered with thin slices of fat pork, moisten with mirepoix and white wine stock, cover with buttered paper and cook them in a moderate oven.

When done, drain off and put them under a weight to get cold, then cover them with either a white or brown *chaudfroid* sauce. Prepare a garnishing composed of cooked channelled mushrooms, carrot balls blanched and cooked in white broth, and seasoned with salt, pepper, oil, vinegar and fine herbs, and some glazed truffle balls. Dress the *chaudfroid* around a bread support covered with ravigote butter, and fill in the intersections with the garnishing; around lay chopped jelly and small cases filled with asparagus tops covered with green mayonnaise with fine herbs. On the top set a round piece of glazed truffle, and around the eases a chain of lozenge-shaped jelly croûtons.

Poularde Adelina Patti

Escoffier's A *Guide to the Art of Modern Cookery* calls for a young chicken to be stuffed with rice and poached in white chicken stock. It is then covered with a sauce made from chicken stock thickened with double cream and surrounded with artichoke bottoms and garnished with a truffle and coated with a pale meat glaze.

Adelina Patti (1843–1919) was a highly acclaimed 19th-century opera singer, earning huge fees at the height of her career in the music capitals of Europe and America.

She was born in Spain to Italian parents and grew up in New York City, where she first sang in public as a child in 1851. She gave her last performance before an audience 63 years later in 1914. Along with her near contemporary Jenny Lind, Patti remains one of the most famous sopranos in history, owing to the purity and beauty of her lyrical voice and the unmatched quality of her *bel canto* technique.

Giuseppe Verdi, writing in 1877, described her as being perhaps the finest singer who had ever lived and a 'stupendous artist'.

In her prime, Patti demanded to be paid $5,000 a night, in gold, before the performance. Her contracts stipulated that her name be given top billing and printed larger than any other name in the cast. Her contracts also insisted that while she was 'free to attend all rehearsals, she was not obligated to attend any'.

In her retirement, Patti, now officially Baroness Cederström, settled in the Swansea Valley in south Wales, where she bought Craig-y-Nos Castle. There she had her own private theatre, a miniature version of the one at Bayreuth, and where she made her gramophone recordings.

Patti also funded the substantial station building at Craig-y-Nos on the Neath and Brecon Railway. In 1918, she presented the Winter Garden building from her Craig-y-Nos estate to the city of Swansea. This was re-erected and renamed the Patti Pavilion. She died at

Craig-y-Nos*, and eight months later, in accordance with the wishes in her will, was buried at the Père Lachaise Cemetery in Paris, to be close to her father and her favourite composer, Rossini.

There still exists a recording of *The Last Rose of Summer* which Patti made in 1905, 43 years after she had sung the same song, at the age of 18, in 1862 to Abraham and Mrs Lincoln.

Chicken Fricassée George Sand

'There is only one happiness in life, to love and be loved.'

This version was developed by the chef Albert Jorant, of La Varenne Cooking School in Paris and named for **George Sand**.

See **Consommé George Sand**, page 39.

---

* The castle is said to be haunted not only by Patti's ghost but also by those of her second husband, the French tenor Nicolini, and the object of her affection, the composer Rossini. Unexplained presences taking many different forms have allegedly been experienced by visitors all over the castle.

CHICKEN

For four

5 tablespoons of unsalted butter
2 tablespoons of safflower oil
1 small carrot, peeled, chopped
1 small onion, minced
1 bay leaf
½ teaspoon of thyme
⅔ lb of medium or small prawns, shelled and deveined
Salt, freshly ground pepper
2 tablespoons of cognac or brandy
½ cup dry white wine
1 cup of chicken stock
½ lb of mushrooms, sliced
1 chicken (3–4 lb), cut into 8 pieces
1½ tablespoons of flour
⅓ cup of whipping cream
2 tablespoons of freshly chopped parsley

Heat 1 tablespoon each of butter and oil in a sauté pan. Add the carrot and onion. Cook until tender and lightly coloured, about 5 minutes. Add the garlic, bay leaf, thyme, prawns, salt and pepper to taste. Continue cooking for about 2 minutes, tossing from time to time.

Carefully add the cognac and light it with a match to flame the prawns and get rid of the alcohol. When the flames have subsided add the wine and stock. Heat to simmer and cook for 3 minutes. With a slotted spoon, transfer the prawns to a warm dish. Continue cooking the liquid until it's reduced to 1 cup. Strain through a sieve into a saucepan, pressing down on the vegetables to extract their juices, then discard the vegetables.

Melt 3 tablespoons of butter in a sauté pan and sauté the mushrooms for 8 minutes. They will absorb the butter, then render their juices; when the juices have cooked away and they start to brown they are ready. Use a slotted spoon to transfer them to the prawns.

Season the chicken with salt and pepper. Heat the remaining butter and oil in pan and sauté the chicken. Transfer the chicken to a platter with the prawns and mushrooms and cover loosely with foil.

Heat the stock in a saucepan. Pour off all but 1½ tablespoons of fat from the sauté pan. Add the flour and cook over low heat for 2 minutes. Off the heat add the stock; heat to boil. Boil for 2 minutes, whisking to remove any lumps. Add the cream and return to boil, stirring for 2 minutes. Season to taste with salt and pepper. Add any juices that have accumulated in the platter. If making the dish in advance put a piece of plastic wrap tightly against the sauce to prevent a skin from forming; reheat before serving.

To serve, spoon sauce over chicken and sprinkle it with parsley.

Chicken à la Stanley

Chicken with onion and cream, garnished with sautéed banana.

Sir Henry Morton Stanley GCB (1841–1904), born John Rowlands, was a Welsh journalist and explorer famous for his exploration of central Africa and his search for the missionary and explorer David Livingstone.

See **Eggs Stanley**, page 173.

Recipe

(From *The Boston Cooking-School Cook Book*, by Fannie Merritt Farmer)

Melt one-fourth cup butter, add one large onion thinly sliced, and two broilers cut in pieces for serving; cover, and cook slowly ten minutes; then add one cup chicken stock, and cook until meat is tender. Remove chickens, rub stock and onions through a sieve, and add one and one-half tablespoons each butter and flour cooked together. Add cream to make sauce of the right consistency. Season with salt and pepper. Arrange chicken on serving dish, pour around sauce, and garnish dish with bananas cut in diagonal slices dipped in flour and sautéed in butter.

Chicken Tettrazzini

Tettrazzini is an American dish most often made with diced chicken, turkey or seafood, with mushrooms and almonds in a butter (or cream) and parmesan sauce, flavoured with wine or sherry, and stock vegetables such as onions, celery, and carrots. It is often served with spaghetti or some similarly thin pasta, garnished with lemon or parsley, and topped with parmesan cheese.

Alternatively, a Tetrazzini can be a baked noodle casserole, sometimes with a browned crust. Recipes for home cooking often use canned cream of mushroom, or other cream soups.

It is widely believed to have been invented between 1908 and 1910 by Ernest Arbogast, the chef at the Palace Hotel in San Francisco, California, where **Luisa Tetrazzini** was a long-time resident. However, other sources attribute the origin to the Knickerbocker Hotel in New York.

Luisa Tettrazzini (1871–1941) was an Italian coloratura soprano known as the 'Florentine Nightingale'. Her voice was remarkable for its phenomenal flexibility, thrust, steadiness and thrilling tone. From the 1890s through to the 1920s, she enjoyed a highly successful operatic and concert career in Europe and America, but her final years were marred by poverty and ill health.

She also featured in E.M. Forster's first novel *Where Angels Fear to Tread* (1905) as a perspiring Italian lady who insists on keeping the windows open in a train, causing one of the characters to get smut in her eye. She then turns up as *Lucia di Lammermoor* on the stage in the Monteriano Opera House. The incidents apparently happened to Forster and his mother while they were making the trip that inspired the book.

In 1920, the McAlpin Hotel on Herald Square in New York City hosted what may have been the first broadcast from a New York hotel. The Army Signal Corps arranged the broadcast by Tetrazzini from her room there. Tetrazzini supposedly gave her recipe for Spaghetti Tetrazzini to Louis Paquet, the executive chef of the McAlpin Hotel. Tetrazzini would subsequently take cooking lessons from Paquet to learn how to make his Spaghetti Tetrazzini before embarking on one of her concert tours.

Chicken Raphael Weill

Raphael Weill (1837–1920) was a pioneer San Francisco merchant who emigrated from France and arrived in San Francisco in 1855, aged 18. Within three years, he had become a partner in the J.W. Davidson Dry Goods Store. By 1885, the Davidson Dry Goods Store had become Raphael Weill and Company, and the store The White House. Widely known for its fine merchandise and excellent employer-employee relations, The White House moved three times before it closed in 1966.

Weill, noted for his civic and philanthropic activities, helped found the Bohemian Club, contributed clothing for victims of the 1906 San Francisco earthquake, was a member of the San Francisco Board of Education, and supported San Francisco's French Hospital, where a wing in the building bears his name. He also contributed to the French community in San Francisco, as well as those living abroad, and he received the French *Legion d'honneur*. A San Francisco public school was named in his honour, and a Rodin statue at the San Francisco Palace of the Legion of Honour was also dedicated to him.

Today he is still remembered in San Francisco restaurants with **Chicken Raphael Weill**.

Recipe

 2 lb chicken
 ½ a lemon
 Salt and freshly ground pepper to taste
 Flour for dredging
 ¼ of a cup of butter
 3 spring onions, chopped
 ½ a cup of dry white wine
 2 tablespoons of chicken stock
 1 egg yolk

CHICKEN

1 cup of double cream
⅛ of a teaspoon of nutmeg
Pinch of cayenne pepper
2 tablespoons of chopped chives
¼ of a cup of chopped parsley
1 tablespoon of tarragon (optional)

Cut the chicken into serving pieces. Rub the pieces with lemon and sprinkle with salt and pepper. Dredge pieces in the flour.

Heat the butter in a heavy skillet and sauté the chicken until golden on all sides. Cover and simmer 10 minutes. Add the scallions and cook five minutes longer shaking the skillet frequently.

Add the wine and simmer two minutes. Add the chicken broth and cook, covered, over low heat for 10 minutes or until the chicken is fork-tender shaking the skillet frequently. Do not boil.

Meanwhile, beat egg yolks with heavy cream and add nutmeg, cayenne, chives and parsley and if desired, tarragon.

Just before serving, pour cream mixture over chicken in pan. Cook over very low heat, stirring or shaking pan constantly until sauce thickens. Arrange chicken on a warm platter and pour the sauce over. Serve at once.

Yield 4–6 servings.

EGGS

Eggs Benedict

An original American breakfast comprising poached eggs
on muffins with a Hollandaise Sauce.

There are several conflicting accounts of the origin of **Eggs Benedict**:

In an interview in the 'Talk of the Town' column of *The New Yorker* in 1942, the year before his death, the retired Wall Street stockbroker **Lemuel Benedict** claimed that in 1894 he had wandered into the Waldorf Hotel and, hoping to find a cure for his morning hangover, had ordered 'buttered toast, poached eggs, crisp bacon, and a hooker of Hollandaise'. Oscar Tschirky, the famed *maître d'hôtel*, was so impressed with the dish that he put it on the hotel's breakfast and lunch menus, but substituted ham for the bacon and a toasted English muffin for the toast.

However, it should be noted that before serving as *maître d'hôtel* at the Waldorf (from 1893 to 1943), Tschirky was on the staff of Delmonico's along with the renowned chef Charles Ranhofer, who in his book *The Epicurean* included 'a selection of interesting bills of fare of Delmonico's from 1862–1894'. This included a recipe for

Eggs Benedict (see below). During Ranhofer's years at Delmonico's, a **Captain and Mrs Le Grand Benedict** were frequent diners there. Five generations of Benedict family members have independently cited similar stories from the late 1860s, that Mrs Benedict became uninterested in the usual Delmonico menu offerings and asked the chef to create 'something new'. He replied, asking if she had any ideas, to which she suggested what is now known as Eggs Benedict (although her original version included a truffle).

Oscar Tschirky quite possibly learned of Eggs Benedict from Ranhofer during their years together at Delmonico's. While Lemuel Benedict may indeed have requested the egg concoction from Tschirky at the Waldorf in 1894, the recipe was already printed in Ranhofer's *The Epicurean*.

A final claim to be the originator of Eggs Benedict was made by Edward P. Montgomery on behalf of **Commodore E.C. Benedict**. In 1967 Montgomery wrote a letter to then *New York Times* columnist Craig Claiborne, which included a recipe he claimed to have received through his uncle, a friend of the commodore. Commodore Benedict's recipe, by way of Montgomery, varies greatly from Ranhofer's version, particularly in the Hollandaise Sauce preparation, which calls for the addition of a 'hot, hard-cooked egg and ham mixture'.

It has been suggested that Pope Benedict XVI should be the patron saint of putting Hollandaise Sauce on poached eggs.

Recipe

Cut some muffins in halves crosswise, toast them without allowing to brown, then put a round of cooked ham an eighth of an inch thick and of the same diameter as the muffins on each half. Heat in a moderate oven and put a poached egg on each toast. Cover the whole with Hollandaise Sauce.

Omelette Arnold Bennett

'Mother is far too clever to understand anything she does not like.'

The magic ingredient in this most famous omelette is undyed smoked haddock.

Arnold Bennett (1867–1931) was an English novelist and journalist. In all Bennett wrote 38 novels, 37 of which were published in his life time. Two of the novels were set in the Savoy Hotel in London; the first was *The Grand Babylon Hotel*, published in 1902, the second, *Imperial Palace*, published in 1930, was his longest. Bennett wrote the latter while staying at the Savoy, and it was then than the **Omelette Arnold Bennett** was created for him by the hotel.

Eggs Berlioz

(Œufs Berlioz)

'At least I have the modesty to admit that lack of modesty is one of my failings.'

These are oval *croustades* made from a Duchesse potato mixture, browned in the oven, then filled with a *salpiçon* of truffles and mushrooms blended with a thick Madeira Sauce. These are then topped with a soft-boiled or poached egg and lightly covered with a Sauce Suprême (*velouté* enriched with cream). A final, optional touch is to fill the middle of the dish with fried cocks' combs à la Villeroi (poached in *court-boullion* and dredged in breadcrumbs).

Hector Berlioz (1803–69) was a French Romantic composer, best known for his compositions *Symphonie fantastique* and the requiem *Grande messe des morts*.

Berlioz often specified huge orchestral forces for some of his works, and conducted several concerts with more than 1,000 musicians. His influence was critical for the development of Romanticism, especially in composers such as Richard Wagner, Nikolai Rimsky-Korsakov, Franz Liszt, Richard Strauss and Gustav Mahler, to name but five.

In Paris in 1832, a concert including *Symphonie fantastique* was performed before an audience which included Victor Hugo, Alexandre Dumas, Heinrich Heine, Niccolò Paganini, Franz Liszt, Frédéric Chopin, George Sand, Alfred de Vigny, Théophile Gautier, Jules Janin, and the Anglo-Irish actress Harriet Smithson. A few days after the performance, Berlioz and Harriet Smithson were introduced and soon entered into a relationship. Despite Berlioz not understanding spoken English and Harriet not knowing any French, on 3rd October 1833, they were married in a civil ceremony at the British Embassy in Paris, with Liszt as one of the witnesses. The following year their only child Louis Berlioz was born, a source of initial disappointment, anxiety and eventual pride to his father.

Unfortunately for Berlioz, he was soon to discover that living under the same roof as 'The Beloved' was far less appealing than worship from afar. The marriage turned out a disaster as both were prone to violent personality clashes and outbursts of temper.

Eggs in a Mould Bizet

'As a musician I tell you that if you were to suppress adultery, fanaticism, crime, evil, the supernatural, there would no longer be the means for writing one note.'

These eggs are made by lining Dariole moulds with minced pickled tongue and truffle. The eggs are then broken into the moulds, and cooked in a *bain-marie*. When cooked, the eggs are taken out of the mould and put onto artichoke hearts. Sometimes a Perigueux Sauce (truffles and Madeira) is served too.

Georges Bizet (1838–75) was a French composer of the Romantic era. He is best known for his operas in a career cut short by his early death. Bizet achieved few successes before his final work ***Carmen*** (see page 52), which has since, however, become one of the most popular and frequently performed works in the entire opera repertoire[*].

---

[*] And it inspired Noël Coward: '*Carmen* by Bizet, is about as Spanish as the Champs Elysées.' (Opera Notes)

Scrambled Eggs à la Columbus

'The air soft as that of Seville in April, and so fragrant that it was delicious to breathe it.'

A heart-stopping assemblage of eggs, ham, fried blood pudding, and beef brains named in honour of **Christopher Columbus** (1451–1506), the Italian explorer and navigator, credited as the first European to discover the New World.

'Columbus's Egg' refers to a brilliant idea or discovery that seems simple or easy after the fact. The expression refers to an apocryphal story in which Columbus, having been told that discovering the Americas was inevitable and no great accomplishment, challenged his critics to make an egg stand on its tip. After his challengers gave up, Columbus did it himself by tapping the egg on the table to flatten its tip.

EGGS

Omelette Saint Hubert

A gamey omelette with mushrooms.

Named for **Saint Hubert of Liège** (656–727).

Recipe

Fold into an omelette some game meat purée bound with a thick *demi-glace* sauce based on concentrated game stock. Onto the omelette put a row of sliced mushrooms lightly fried in butter. Serve with a ring of *demi-glace* sauce.

See **Game Saint Hubert of Liège**, page 131.

Œufs sur le plat Omer Pasha

Fried eggs with onion, green pepper, tomato and bacon.

Omar Latas or Mihajlo Latas (1806–71), better known as

Omar Pasha, was born in Austrian territory in what is now Croatia. He was initially an Austrian soldier, but when faced with charges of embezzlement, he fled to Ottoman Bosnia and converted to Islam. He then joined the Ottoman army, where he quickly climbed in ranks. He crushed several rebellions throughout the empire, and was a commander in the Crimean War, where he defeated Russia at Sevastopol.

A clear and precise military thinker, Omar Pasha took bold decisions and relentlessly followed them through. Although he had a reputation as a strict and ruthless disciplinarian, he was revered and respected by his men.

Recipe

Melt a little butter on a dish that can go in the oven; when heated, break in twelve eggs, one beside the other, keeping the yolks whole; cook in a moderate oven for five to six minutes. Fry two ounces of chopped onions in butter and as much cut-up green peppers, add three gills of tomato sauce and half the quantity of half-glaze sauce and white wine; reduce this but don't make it too thick. Add finely chopped unsmoked bacon; fry it in butter, moisten with a little Madeira, then reduce a little more. Pour this sauce over the eggs or else serve it in a separate sauce boat.

Eggs Picabia

(Œufs Francis Picabia)

'Only useless things are indispensable.'

Francis Picabia (1879–1953) was a French *avant-garde* poet and painter, a major figure in the Dada movement.

Recipe

(From *The Alice B. Toklas Cookbook**, by Alice B. Toklas)

The only painter who ever gave me a recipe was Francis Picabia, and though it is only a dish of eggs, it merits the name of its creator.

Break 8 eggs into a bowl and mix them well with a fork, add salt but no pepper. Pour them into a saucepan – yes, a saucepan, no, not a frying pan. Put the saucepan over a very, very low flame, keep turning

---

* The *Alice B. Toklas Cookbook* (1953) should not be confused, as it often is, with *The Autobiography of Alice B. Toklas* (1933). Alice B. Toklas herself wrote *The Alice B. Toklas Cookbook*, but Gertrude Stein wrote *The Autobiography of Alice B. Toklas*.

them with a fork while very slowly adding in very small quantities ½ lb butter – not a speck less, rather more if you can bring yourself to it. It should take ½ hour to prepare this dish. The eggs, of course, are not scrambled, but with the butter, no substitute admitted, produce a suave consistency that perhaps only gourmets will appreciate.

Poached Eggs Sévigné

'I dislike clocks with second hands; they cut up life into too small pieces.'

Poached eggs served on a bed of braised lettuce and topped with a Sauce Suprême, this in turn topped with sliced truffles.

Marie de Rabutin-Chantal, Marquise de Sévigné (1626–96) was a French aristocrat, particularly remembered for her letter writing. Most of her letters, celebrated for their wit and vividness, were addressed to her daughter Françoise. Today in France, Madame de Sévigné is thought of as one of the great icons of French literature.

Madame de Sévigné was the first literary lady to have a dish named after her and was meant to be very fond of Burgundy.

Eggs Stanley

These are poached eggs with a sauce made with half a teaspoon of curry powder, named for the legendary **Henry Morton Stanley**.

See **Chicken à la Stanley**, page 155.

Omelette André Theuriet

An omelette made with asparagus, cream, morilles and truffles.

Claude Adhémar André Theuriet (1833–1907) was a distinguished French poet, dramatist and novelist.

Theuriet was made a knight of the *Légion d'honneur* in 1879, and in 1890 received the *prix Vitet* from the Académie française. In 1895 he became an officer of the *Légion d'honneur* and in 1896 a member of the Académie française.

Théophile Gautier compared Theuriet to Jacques in the Forest of Arden from *As You Like It*.

Gautier's poem *Paysage* was set to music by Reynaldo Hahn.

Eggs Rachel

Fried eggs on toast cut into perfect circles and decorated with bone marrow and slices of truffle.

See **Salade Rachel**, page 57, **Tournedos Rachel**, page 95, **Filets de Sole Rachel**, page 187, **Vegetables Rachel**, page 237, and the **Rachel Sandwich**, page 258.

FISH

Red Snapper à la Demidoff

Named for Russian industrialist, diplomat and patron of the arts, **Count Anatoly Nikolaievich Demidov** (1813–70), 1st Prince of San Donato.

See **Chicken Demidoff**, page 144, and **Rissoles à la Demidoff**, page 176.

Recipe

(From *The Epicurean*, by Charles Ranhofer)

Keep the fillets whole while taking them from the fish; remove the skin, pare and cut them up into bias slices, trim these giving them an oval shape, then season and cover the surface with a cream forcemeat. Decorate the tops with truffles, range them in a buttered sautoir, and moisten with fish stock; cover over with buttered paper, and let cook in a slack oven. Reduce the stock with an equal quantity of *velouté* sauce; garnish around the fish with oysters from which the hard parts have been removed, small lobster rissolettes, and very green parsley leaves on each end. Serve the sauce in a separate sauce-boat.

Sole Dugléré

Sole fillets which are folded, poached in white wine and served with a *velouté* sauce, then garnished with tomatoes and parsley.

This is a French dish. 'À *la Dugléré*' indicates a garnish of shallots, onions and tomatoes.

Adolphe Dugléré (1805–84) was a French chef and a pupil of the great Antoine Carême.

Until 1848, Dugléré was a *chef de cuisine* to the Rothschild family. From 1848–66 he was the manager at the restaurant Les Frères Provençaux at the Palais-Royal, which was owned by three men from Provence named Barthélémy, Maneille and Simonas (who weren't, in reality, brothers).

In 1866 Dugléré became the head chef of the Café Anglais, which was the most famous Paris restaurant of the 19th century and where he is believed to have created the dish **Pommes Anna** (see page 230).

It was here, in 1867, that Dugléré served a famous meal that became known as the *Dîner des trois empereurs* (Dinner of the Three Emperors) for Tsar Alexander II of Russia, his son the tsarevich (who later became Tsar Alexander III) and King William I of Prussia, as well as Prince Otto von Bismarck, all of whom were in Paris for *L'Exposition universelle*. The table service used for this meal is on display to this day at the oldest existing restaurant in Paris, the Tour d'Argent, which is owned by the descendants of Claudius Burdet, the last owner of the Café Anglais, which was demolished in 1913.

Dugléré was described as a taciturn and serious person who demanded ingredients of the highest quality and abhorred drunkenness and smoking. He forbade his employees to smoke even outside of the workplace. Nor were customers allowed to smoke until dinner was over, at which time the *maître d'hôtel* went from table to table lighting cigars. Dugléré was a cultivated man and Alexandre Dumas consulted him several times for his *Le Grand Dictionnaire de cuisine* (1871).

Little more is known about him but he did leave some notebooks which are on permanent loan to the National Library in Paris.

The most famous dish attributed to Dugléré is almost certainly Pommes Anna. Other dishes created by Dugléré include Potage Germiny, a sorrel soup created for Charles Lebègue, Comte de Germiny, governor of the Bank of France; **Poularde Albufera** (see page 140); Soufflé à l'anglaise*; Culotte de bœuf Salomon (dedicated to Salomon de Rothschild); Barbue à la Dugléré (brill in tomato and parsley sauce); and of course **Sole Dugléré**.

---

* In response to an enquiry, the Restaurant de la Tour d'Argent, the current trustees of Dugléré's papers, replied that he left no record of the ingredients for this dish.

Filets de soles à la Duse

'If the sight of the blue skies fills you with joy, if a blade of grass springing up in the fields has power to move you, if the simple things of nature have a message that you understand, rejoice, for your soul is alive.'

Fillets of sole made into rounds, the centres stuffed with prawns. These are dressed with a **Mornay Sauce** (see page 225) and decorated with sliced truffle. They are served on a bed of rice.

There is also a Duse Garnish made with green beans, tomatoes, **Potatoes Parmentier** (see page 236) and butter.

Eleonora Duse (1858–1924) was a great and beautiful Italian tragedienne. She was famous for her portrayal of *La Dame aux Camélias*, her affair with Gabriele d'Annunzio, and of course for inspiring the unknown chef who created **Filets de soles à la Duse.**

Flounder Jules Janin

(Plies carrelets ou limandes à la Jules Janin)

Gabriel-Jules Janin (1804–74) was a writer, theatre critic and friend of Berlioz and Dumas. He is remembered as an eccentric and the author of the novel *L'Âne mort et la Femme guillotinée* (The Dead Donkey and the Guillotined Woman), published in 1829. This was the second of the 38 books written by Janin and published in his lifetime.

Recipe

(From *The Epicurean*, by Charles Ranhofer)

Remove the fillets from the flounders, from these remove the black skin, season, cover with a quenelle forcemeat, pare, and fold them in two; lay these fillets on a buttered dish, moisten with white wine, pour over some butter, and set the dish in the oven. When they are done drain them into a *sautoir*, straining the liquid; reduce this with an Espagnole Sauce and Madeira; garnish the fish ranged in a circle with oysters, sliced truffles, and crayfish tails. Butter the sauce, pass it through a tammy, and pour it over the whole.

Trout Joan of Arc

(Truites à la Jeanne d'Arc)

'I am not afraid... I was born to do this.'

Joan of Arc (1412–31), nicknamed 'the Maid of Orléans', was born in Domrémy, in the Duchy of Bar in France. Joan cropped her hair, wore men's clothing and remained a virgin, gaining mythical status among her followers. At the age of 18, Joan led the French army to victory over the British at Orléans. She was captured a year later, on 30th May 1431, and was burned as a heretic by the English and their French collaborators.

Twenty-five years after her execution, an inquisitorial court authorised by Pope Callixtus III examined the trial, pronounced Joan innocent, and declared her a martyr. She was beatified in 1909 and canonised as a Roman Catholic saint on 16th May 1920.

She is a national heroine of France and one of the nine secondary patron saints of France, along with Saint Denis, Saint Martin of Tours, Saint Louis, Saint Michael, Saint Remi, Saint Petronilla, Saint Radegund and Saint Thérèse of Lisieux.

Recipe

Remove the fillets and skin from several quarter of a pound trout, put them in a dish and season them with salt, pepper, oil, vinegar, a bay leaf, parsley and finely chopped onions. Let the fish marinate for two hours, then take them out of the dish and dip them in melted butter, roll them in breadcrumbs and fry them gently. Finally sprinkle them with cayenne butter and serve with a *velouté* sauce finished with crayfish butter and lemon juice.

Filets de Sole Marguery

Nicolas Marguery (1834–1910) began his career as a dishwasher at the Restaurant Champeaux in Paris, during which time he married the restaurant owner's daughter. Next he became an apprentice chef at the Rocher de Concale and then at the Frères Provençeaux. In 1887 he opened his own restaurant in Paris on the Boulevard Bonne-Nouvelle, which he aptly called the Marguery. This soon became a great rendezvous for gourmands. It was famous for its cellar and **Filets de Sole Marguery**, served with mussels and prawns.

Today in Paris you will find the Restaurant Au Petit Marguery at 9 Boulevard de Port-Royal.

Lord Nelson Sole

(Filets de soles Nelson)

Poached sole fillets with white wine sauce presented with a pyramid of potato balls. A form of fish-and-chips.

See **Lord Nelson Veal**, page 108, and **Spring Lamb Cutlets Nelson**, page 118.

Recipe

(From *Guide to the Art of Modern Cookery*, by Auguste Escoffier)

Fold the fillets, and poach them in fish fumet. Arrange them in a circle on a dish; coat them with white wine sauce, and glaze quickly. Garnish the centre of the dish with a pyramid of potato balls cooked in butter and of a light-brown colour. Surround the fillets with poached milt.

Sole Picasso

'My mother said to me, "If you are a soldier, you will become a general. If you are a monk, you will become the Pope." Instead, I was a painter, and became Picasso.'

The dish consists of fried or grilled sole served with warm fruit in a ginger and lemon sauce.

Pablo Picasso (1881–1973) was a Spanish painter and sculptor, also a printmaker, ceramicist, stage designer and poet. He is perhaps the most famous and influential artist of the 20th century.

When you consider his full name, Pablo Diego José Francisco de Paula Juan Nepomuceno María de los Remedios Cipriano de la Santísima Trinidad Ruiz y Picasso, you understand why he signed his work with just one.

Sole Marco Polo

'I have not told half of what I saw.'

This is fillets of sole with lobster and, somewhat incongruously, tomato.

Marco Polo (1254–1324) was a great Venetian explorer and merchant traveller.

He was the author of *Il Milione* ('the million'), in English commonly called *The Travels of Marco Polo*, a 13th-century travelogue written down in Old French by Rustichello da Pisa, working from accounts which he had heard from Marco Polo when they were imprisoned together in Genoa. It describes Polo's travels through Asia, Persia, China, and Indonesia between 1276 and 1291, and his experiences at the court of Kublai Khan.

Lamprey à la Rabelais

'If the skies fall, one may hope to catch larks.'

François Rabelais (c. 1483–1553) was a major French Renaissance humanist and writer, as well as a monk, a doctor, a professor of anatomy, and Greek scholar. His best known works are *Pantagruel* (1532) and *Gargantua* (1534). Western literary critics consider him one of the great writers of world literature and among the creators of modern European writing.

In France, the moment at a restaurant when the waiter presents the bill is still sometimes called '*le quart d'heure de Rabelais*', in memory of a famous trick Rabelais used to get out of paying a tavern bill when he had no money, as described below by Edward Rothstein:

'Before sitting down at an inn to eat a meal he couldn't pay for and setting off on a journey to Paris he couldn't afford, the destitute Rabelais ostentatiously put aside a few packages that were sure to attract attention. They were labelled "poison for the king" and "poison for the dauphin". When, after the meal, the innkeeper found them, he immediately had Rabelais arrested and transported to Paris, where he was welcomed by the king with hearty laughter at the free trip and the bill-avoiding scheme.'

Recipe

(From *The Epicurean*, by Charles Ranhofer)

Bleed the lamprey, reserving the blood, and mix it in with a little vinegar; cut the fish into slices, fry them in butter adding chopped onions, salt, sugar, and allspice; dredge over with a little flour, moisten with white wine, and lay in a bunch of parsley garnished with thyme and bay leaf, also small glazed onions; let cook from twelve to fifteen minutes. Dress the lampreys and the small onions, thicken the sauce with the blood and then strain it through a tammy ; cover the fish with this sauce, and surround the lampreys with fluted mushroom heads fried in butter, and seasoned with salt, pepper, and fine herbs; range round the whole very thin sliced lemon.

Filets de Sole Rachel

Sole fillets rolled into crowns which are then filled with asparagus tips and garnished with slices of truffle.

See **Salade Rachel**, page 57, **Tournedos Rachel**, page 95, **Eggs Rachel**, page 174, **Vegetables Rachel**, page 237, and the **Rachel Sandwich**, page 258.

Paupiettes Réjane

Whiting fillets with watercress butter, slices of Jerusalem artichoke and bone marrow.

See **Salade Réjane**, page 58.

Fillets of Brill Véron

Dr Louis Désiré Véron (1798–1867) gave up his Parisian medical practice for the more fashionable life of a writer, manager of the Opéra, paramour of the actress Rachel, political influence, and pre-eminent host of lavish dinners for the élite.

Véron originally made his fortune from patent medicines. In 1829 he founded the literary magazine *Revue de Paris*, and from 1838–52 was owner and director of *Le Constitutionnel*, in which he published Eugène Sue's novel, *Le juif errant*, based on the legend of the Wandering Jew.

Véron is largely known to history for his direction, from 1831–35, of the Paris Opéra. After the July Revolution of 1830, the new government wanted to offload the costs and responsibilities of the Opéra, which had been effectively state-controlled since its inception. Véron saw the great potential of adapting the Opéra to the bourgeois tastes of new audiences and applied for the franchise, which brought with it a limited state subsidy. By bringing together the talents of designers (such as Duponchel), composers (such as Meyerbeer, Auber and Fromental Halévy), and librettists (such as Eugène Scribe and Casimir Delavigne), and developing great singers such as Adolphe Nourrit and Cornélie Falcon, he created the genre of Grand Opera. The first new production under Véron's management, Meyerbeer's *Robert le diable* (21st November 1831) began a new era in opera. When, in 1835, the government decided to further reduce its subsidy of the Opéra, Véron prudently withdrew, having made a substantial profit.

Recipe

(From the *Larousse Gastronomique*)

Cut the fillets in half lengthways, season with salt and pepper, dip in melted butter and breadcrumbs, sprinkle with more melted butter, and cook gently under the grill. Arrange the fillets on a hot serving dish and coat with **Sauce Véron** (see page 228).

Sole Véronique

Véronique is an *opéra comique* (operetta) by André Messager (1853–1929). It was first performed at the Théâtre des Bouffes Parisiens, in Paris, on 10th December 1898, and in London in 1903. The operetta involves a great deal of disguise and deception and much fun and flirting by Hélène de Solanges and her aunt Emerance. In her pursuit of and flirting with Florestan, Vicomte de Valaincourt, Hélène disguises herself as the flower girl Véronique. All is eventually revealed and untangled, leading to a not unexpected happy ending.

It was to celebrate its London opening at the Coronet Theatre in Notting Hill Gate that Auguste Escoffier created **Sole Véronique**.

Recipe

(From the BBC)

  10 g of butter, plus extra for greasing
  4 x 200 g/7 oz of skinless sole fillets
  200 ml/7 fl oz of fresh fish stock
  100 ml/3½ fl oz of dry vermouth
  1 bay leaf
  150 ml/5 fl oz of double cream

200 g/7 oz of green grapes, cut in half and deseeded (perhaps even peeled)
Flaked sea salt and freshly ground white pepper

Preheat the oven to 180°C/350°F/Gas Mark 4.

Lightly butter a shallow ovenproof dish. Fold the fish fillets in half and put in a single layer in the dish. Dot them with pieces of butter.

Pour the fish stock and vermouth around the fish. Cover the fish with a sheet of buttered aluminium foil. Bake until just cooked, 20 minutes or so.

Remove the fish from the oven and carefully pour the cooking liquid into a large frying pan. Cover the fish with the foil and put back in the oven to keep warm.

Bring the cooking liquor to the boil. Boil it until it's reduced to around 100 ml/3½ fl oz liquid. Pour the cream into the pan and return it to a simmer. Stir in the grapes. Cook until the grapes are hot, perhaps a further minute.

Season with salt and freshly ground white pepper. Remove the fish from the oven and gently pour the sauce over it.

Serve immediately.

Fillets of Sole Walewska

Sole fillets poached in a fish fumet, garnished with slices of lobster and truffle, and served with a Mornay Sauce.

Alexandre Florian Joseph, Count Colonna-Walewski (1810–68), was a Polish and French politician and diplomat. He was widely rumoured to be the (unacknowledged) illegitimate son of Napoleon I by his mistress, Countess Marie Walewska. However, Countess Walewska's husband legally acknowledged him as his son. He had two children by his first wife and four by his second. He also had a son by the actress Rachel.

Walewski was French ambassador at London and Minister for Foreign Affairs under Napoleon III.

SEAFOOD

~

Lobster and Crayfish Soup Duke Alexis

(Potage de homard et d'écrevisses au Duc Alexis)

Grand Duke Alexei Alexandrovich of Russia (1850–1908) was the fifth child and the fourth son of Alexander II of Russia and his first wife Maria Alexandrovna. Destined to a naval career, Alexei Alexandrovich started his military training at the age of seven, and perhaps not surprisingly, by the age of 20, had been appointed lieutenant of the Russian Imperial Navy. In the winter of 1871–72 he was sent as a goodwill ambassador to the United States and Japan.

During his grand tour of America, a dinner was held in his honour at Delmonico's Restaurant in New York, which featured what would become **Lobster and Crayfish Soup Duke Alexis**.

Recipe

(From *The Epicurean*, by Charles Ranhofer)

Mince finely some carrots, onions and celery; fry them in butter, and moisten with one quart of white wine and two quarts of broth, adding four peeled tomatoes cut in two and pressed. Put into this stock eighteen crayfish, let them boil for five minutes, then lift them out, and put in four pounds of live lobsters, selecting the smallest ones procurable, and cook them for half an hour, then drain them, and pick out all their meals, keeping aside only the meat from the claws, and pounding the rest; dilute this with the above stock, adding one quart of thickened fish soup stock; strain through a sieve and heat up to boiling point, but do not allow it to boil, thicken it with raw egg-yolks, cream and fine butter, the proportion being two raw egg-yolks, one gill of cream and two ounces of fine butter for each quart of soup. Detach the tails from the bodies of the crayfish; suppress the belly side so as to keep only the thin shells of the bodies, and stuff these with the crayfish meat, chopped up fine and mixed in with an equal quantity of fish forcemeat made with crayfish, butter, season well, and poach them in boiling, salted water.

Put these stuffed bodies into the soup as garnishing, and if too large cut them in two lengthwise.

Lobster Paul Bert

(Homard à la Paul Bert)

Paul Bert (1833–86) was a French zoologist, physiologist and politician. He entered the École polytechnique at Paris intending to become an engineer, then changed his mind, studied law, and finally took up physiology.

After the Paris Commune of 1870 he began to take part in politics as a supporter of Gambetta. In 1874 he was elected to the Assembly, where he sat on the extreme left, and in 1876 to the Chamber of Deputies.

From November 1881 to January 1882, Bert was minister of education and worship in Gambetta's short-lived cabinet, and in a Paris theatre in 1881 he created a great sensation with a lecture on modern Catholicism, in which he poured ridicule on the fables and follies of the chief religious tracts and handbooks that circulated especially in the south of France. Early in 1886 he was appointed resident-general in Annam and Tonkin, and died of dysentery at Hanoi on 11th November that year.

Bert was more distinguished as a man of science than as a politician or administrator. His classical work, *La Pression barometrique* (1878) is a comprehensive investigation on the physiological effects of air pressure, both above and below the normal. Central nervous system oxygen toxicity was first described in this publication and is sometimes referred to as the 'Paul Bert effect'. He showed that oxygen was toxic to insects, arachnids, myriapods, molluscs, earthworms, fungi, germinating seeds, birds, and other animals.

Recipe

(From *The Epicurean*, by Charles Ranhofer)

Take eight one-pound lobsters and plunge them into boiling water into which has been added a bunch of parsley, sliced onions, salt, pepper and vinegar; let them boil steadily twenty minutes, then remove; detach the bodies from the tails; take the meat out whole from the latter, breaking the inside of the shell only; then wash and dry the shells. Cut up the tail meat into transversal slices; put four ounces of butter into a *sautoir*, range the lobster escalops on top, and sauté them, adding a small finely chopped up shallot, half as much shrimps as lobster, and half as much fresh, peeled walnuts as shrimps. (Should there be no fresh walnuts procurable, take dry ones and soak them for twelve hours in salt and water, then peel.) Drain off the butter and replace it by a reduced Béchamel Sauce thickened with egg-yolks, cream and fresh butter, with lemon juice and chopped parsley, being careful to have the sauce quite thick. Fill the lobster shells with this preparation, dress them crown-shaped on a bed of parsley, and arrange a bunch of parsley leaves on top.

Oysters Bienville

This consists of oysters on the half shell topped with a **Béchamel Sauce** (see page 217) flavoured with sherry and cayenne pepper and mixed with sautéed garlic, shallots, mushrooms and prawns. A mixture of breadcrumbs and grated cheese is sprinkled over the top and the oysters are baked on a bed of rock salt until browned and bubbling.

Jean-Baptiste Le Moyne de Bienville (1680–1767) was four times governor of Louisiana (1701–43) and the founder of New Orleans.

In 1717 Bienville wrote to the directors of The Company of the West that he had discovered a crescent bend in the Mississippi River which he felt was safe from tidal surges and hurricanes and suggested that the new capital of the colony be built there. Permission was granted, and on 7th May 1718 Bienville founded New Orleans. In 1720 following disagreements with the chief engineer of the colony, Pierre Le Blond de la Tour, Bienville ordered an assistant engineer, Adrien de Pauger, to draw up plans for the new city. In 1721, Pauger designed the eleven-by-seven block rectangle now known as the French Quarter or the *Vieux Carré*. After moving into his new home on the site of what is now the Custom House, Bienville named the new city 'La Nouvelle-Orléans' in honour of Philippe II, Duke of Orléans, prince regent of France. By 1723, New Orleans became the capital of French Louisiana.

Oysters Bienville was created in the late 1930s by a Frenchman named 'Count' Arnaud Cazenave at his restaurant, Arnaud's, in the French Quarter of New Orleans.

The Germaine Cazenave Wells Mardi Gras Museum, named after the successor to and daughter of Count Arnaud, opened in the French Quarter restaurant on 15th September 1983. Wells reportedly reigned as Queen of over 22 Mardi Gras balls from 1937 to 1968, more than any other woman in the history of Carnival.

Shrimp De Jonghe's

Shrimp De Jonghe's is a specialty of Chicago. It is a casserole of whole peeled prawns in soft, garlicky, sherry-laced bread crumbs. It can be served as an appetiser or a main course. It has the oldest pedigree of Chicagoan cuisine, having originated in the late 19th or early 20th century at De Jonghe's Hotel and Restaurant. The recipe has been attributed to the owners, the brothers **Henri, Pierre and Charles De Jonghe**, Belgian immigrants who went to Chicago to run a restaurant at the World's Columbian Exposition (1893), or to their chef, **Emil Zehr**. However it does look as if Zehr should get the credit, as explained in an article from the *Chicago Tribune*, dated 21st February 1985:

'Shrimp De Jonghe, or is it De Zehr?

Ever heard of Shrimp Zehr? That's what a Chicagoan said Shrimp De Jonghe should be called, because his father invented it more than 70 years ago.

Emil G. Zehr got in touch with *The Tribune* last month after reading a recipe and story in the Sunday magazine about the classic shrimp dish served at De Jonghe's Restaurant in the early 1900s. The story mentioned that chef, Emil Zehr – our reader's father – developed the recipe.

But Emil G. said that the recipe we ran isn't the original. (We didn't say it was the original.) "Dad would never have used liquor in his recipe," Zehr's son said. "There have been a lot of recipes published, but only his is the original."

He offered to share his father's original recipe, which appears below. If cooking shrimp for 16–21 minutes seems extreme, remember that the recipe was invented shortly after the turn of the century. Shrimp may not have been pristinely fresh then and certainly tastes have changed. Cooking time could easily be reduced and the recipe could be cut in half for a smaller sampling. We didn't test this recipe, but we've added a few words to the directions for clarification. Extra butter mixture will keep refrigerated for several days or can be frozen for several weeks or amounts can be reduced.'

Recipe

In the UK, remember, for 'shrimp', read 'prawns'.

For four

Butter mixture

- 14 cups of homemade white breadcrumbs, see step 1
- 3 cups of homemade brown breadcrumbs, see step 1
- 2 lb of butter
- 1 lb of margarine
- ⅓ of a cup of chopped shallots

1 tablespoon of Worcestershire Sauce
3 drops of liquid hot pepper sauce
1 cup of chopped fresh garlic
1 cup of chopped parsley

Shrimp

12 large shrimp

1. Make your breadcrumbs from French or Italian bread, 3 days old. This has a great deal to do with its fine texture when finished.

2. Knead the butter and margarine until soft. Add the remaining ingredients, except shrimp, to butter mixture. Mix well in a wooden bowl. Form into sausage-like form and put it in the refrigerator to set.

3. Cover the bottom of a casserole with eighth-inch slices of butter mixture. Put 12 large shrimp which have been cooked for 6 minutes, peeled and cleaned, on top of the butter mixture slices. Cover the shrimp with quarter–inch slices of butter mixture. Put in a hot oven (375° to 400°) and bake until the breadcrumbs are brown, 10 to 15 minutes.

Coquilles St. Jacques

Coquilles St. Jacques is the French term for scallops; the 'St. Jacques' was **Saint James the Great**, son of Zebedee, who died in 44 AD.

The scallop shell is the traditional emblem of James and is very much associated with pilgrims on the Way of Saint James to the apostle's shrine at Santiago de Compostela in Galicia, Spain. Medieval Christians making the pilgrimage often wore a scallop-shell symbol on their hat or clothes. The pilgrim also carried a scallop shell with him, and would present himself at churches, castles, abbeys and houses, where he could expect to be given as much sustenance as he could pick up with one scoop. Thus even the poorest household could give charity without being overburdened. Probably the pilgrim would have been given oats or barley, and perhaps beer or wine.

The association of Saint James with the scallop can probably be traced to the legend that the apostle once rescued a knight covered in scallops. Another version of the legend holds that while Saint James' remains were being transported from Jerusalem to Galicia, a knight's horse fell into the sea, and emerged covered in the shells.

Shrimp Lamaze

Shrimp Lamaze is a very American recipe. They say 'shrimp' when we say 'prawns'. The recipe includes 'India relish' which is something like Piccalilli, and 'A-1 sauce' which, from the design of the label, you might think is the same as HP Sauce but isn't.

Shrimp Lamaze was developed by the chef Johann Lamprecht at the *Warwick Hotel* in Philadelphia. It was named after the owner of the hotel, **George Lamaze**, who died in 1940.

Recipe

For four

2 cups of mayonnaise
½ cup of India relish
2 cups of chilli sauce
1 tablespoon of prepared mustard
1 teaspoon of chopped chives
1 hardboiled egg, peeled, chopped and chilled
Salt and pepper to taste
Dash of A-1 sauce
2 lb of shrimp, cooked and shelled

Use a chilled bowl. Combine the mayonnaise, relish, chilli sauce, mustard, chives and egg. Season with salt, pepper and A-1 sauce. Serve the sauce over cold, cooked shrimp, or other seafood, on a bed of red leaf lettuce that has been soaked in iced water.

Oyster Omelette Jenny Lind

See **Jenny Lind Soup**, page 30.

Recipe

For two or three

  6 large oysters, shelled. Reserve their liquor
  4 eggs, separated
  1 tablespoon of single cream
  Dash of cayenne pepper
  Salt and pepper to taste
  2–3 tablespoons of butter

Poach the oysters in their own liquor until their edges start to curl, 2 or 3 minutes. Drain them well and then cut them into pieces.

Combine the egg yolks, cream, cayenne pepper, salt and pepper. Beat the mixture lightly with a fork, then mix in the oyster bits. Stiffly beat the egg whites and then fold them into the oyster mixture.

Heat the butter in an omelette pan until it sizzles. Pour in the egg mixture and reduce the heat slightly. As the omelette cooks, lift it with a spatula, letting the uncooked part run under, until the whole is creamy. Fold the omelette double and cook it for half a minute more. Turn it out onto a hot plate.

Crab Louie (or Louis)

The main ingredient for **Crab Louie**, as the names suggests, is crab meat. The preferred crab is Dungeness Crab, but other crab meat can be substituted. Although variations of the recipe do exist, an essential ingredient is a creamy dressing such as Louis Dressing (see below), Thousand Island Dressing or Green Goddess Dressing. The dressing is either served on the side or mixed with the other ingredients.

The exact origins of this dish are uncertain.

In 1908 the menu for Bergez-Frank's Old Poodle Dog restaurant in San Francisco included 'Crab Leg à la Louis (special)'. This was named after the chef **Louis Coutard,** who had died that year.

There's also a 'Crabmeat à la Louise Salad' in the 1910 edition of a cookery book by the head chef of the city's St. Francis Hotel,

Victor Hirtzler.

Another early recipe is in the *The Neighborhood Cook Book*, compiled by the Portland Council of Jewish Women in 1912.

It is known that Crab Louie was being served at Solari's restaurant in San Francisco as early as 1914. There's also a recipe for it from this date in a publication entitled *Bohemian San Francisco* by Clarence E. Edwords.

Some accounts say the dish was created by the entrepreneur and founder of the Davenport Hotel in Spokane, Washington, **Louis Davenport**. Davenport spent his early years in San Francisco before moving to Spokane Falls. He would use crab imported from Seattle. His recipe pre-dates 1914 and can be found in historic hotel menus.

The popularity of Crab Louie has diminished since its heyday in the early to mid-1900s, but it can still be found on the menus of some hotels and restaurants on the West Coast, including the Palace Hotel in San Francisco.

Recipe

A typical Crab Louie Salad consists of:

Crab meat
Hardboiled eggs
Tomato
Asparagus

Other ingredients such as olives and spring onion have also been listed as ingredients in some recipes. It is served on a bed of Iceberg lettuce.

Louis Dressing is a salad dressing based on mayonnaise, to which have been added red chilli sauce, finely chopped spring onions and finely chopped green chilli peppers.

Lobster Newberg

(Homard à la Newberg)

An American dish made with lobster, butter, cream, cognac, sherry, eggs, and cayenne pepper.

Lobster Newberg (also spelled 'Lobster Newburg') was invented by a sea captain in the fruit trade between Cuba and New York, **Ben Wenberg**. In 1876 he demonstrated it to the manager at Delmonico's Restaurant in New York City, Charles Delmonico. After refinements by Delmonico's chef, Charles Ranhofer, the creation was added to the restaurant's menu as 'Lobster à la Wenberg' and soon became very popular.

It wasn't long before an argument between Wenberg and Charles Delmonico caused the dish to be removed from the menu. However, to satisfy patrons' continued requests for it, Delmonico changed the name, by means of a simple anagram, to 'Lobster à la Newberg' or simply 'Lobster Newberg'.

When Ranhofer's recipe first appeared in print in 1894, the lobsters were boiled for 25 minutes, then fried in clarified butter, then simmered in cream until the cream had reduced by half, and then brought to the boil again after the addition of Madeira.

Recipe

(From *The Epicurean*, by Charles Ranhofer)

Cook six lobsters, each weighing about two pounds, in boiling salted water for twenty-five minutes. Twelve pounds of live lobster when cooked yields from two to two and a half pounds of meat and three to four ounces of lobster coral. When cold, detach the bodies from the tails and cut the latter into slices, put them into a *sautoir*, each piece lying flat and add hot clarified butter; season with salt and fry lightly on both sides without colouring; moisten to their height with good raw cream; reduce quickly to half and then add two or three spoonfuls of Madeira wine; boil the liquid once more only, then remove and thicken with a thickening of egg-yolks and fresh cream. Cook without boiling, incorporating a little cayenne and butter; warm it up again without boiling, tossing the lobster lightly, then arrange the pieces in a vegetable dish and pour the sauce over.

Oysters Rockefeller

'Don't blame the marketing department. The buck stops with the chief executive.'

Oysters Rockefeller, one of New Orleans' most famous dishes, was created in 1899 by Jules Alciatore, the son of the founder of Antoine's Restaurant. He named his creation after the tycoon **John D. Rockefeller** (1839–1937). It is a dish of baked oysters on the half shell topped with a very rich (like Rockefeller) sauce and served on a bed of rock salt.

The original recipe is still a secret. However the sauce is known to be a purée of a number of green vegetables other than spinach. Jules Alciatore developed Oysters Rockefeller in the face of a shortage of French snails by substituting locally available oysters of which there were, and still are, a great many. Antoine's has been serving Oysters Rockefeller, using the original recipe, since 1899.

It is estimated that since then, they have served more than three and a half million orders. If each order contained just six oysters, that would mean 21 million oysters. With a dozen oysters per order the total is (obviously) twice that – 42 million.

Recipe

(From www.epicurious.com)

In absence of the original recipe, this lighter take features spinach, watercress, spring onions and grated parmesan.

1 garlic clove
2 cups of loosely packed fresh spinach
1 bunch of watercress, stems trimmed
½ a cup of chopped spring onions
¾ of a cup of unsalted butter, at room temperature
½ a cup of dry breadcrumbs
2 tablespoons of Pernod or other anise-flavoured liqueur
1 teaspoon of fennel seeds, ground
1 teaspoon of hot pepper sauce
About 1 pound of rock salt
24 fresh oysters, shucked, shells reserved
¼ of a cup of freshly grated parmesan

Position rack in top third of oven and preheat to 450°F. Finely chop garlic in processor. Add spinach, watercress and spring onions to garlic. Process, using on/off turns, until mixture is finely chopped. Transfer mixture to medium bowl.

Combine the butter, breadcrumbs, Pernod, fennel and hot sauce in processor. Process until well blended. Return spinach mixture to the processor. Process, using on/off turns, just until mixtures are blended.

Season with salt and pepper. (Can be made 8 hours ahead. Cover; chill.)

Sprinkle rock salt over large baking sheet to depth of ½ an inch. Arrange the oysters in half shells on the rock salt. Top each oyster with 1 tablespoon of the spinach mixture. Sprinkle with cheese. Bake until the spinach mixture browns on top, about 8 minutes.

Lobster Cutlets à la Shelley

'When my cats aren't happy, I'm not happy. Not because I care about their mood but because I know they're just sitting there thinking up ways to get even.'

Percy Bysshe Shelley (1792–1822) was one of the major English Romantic poets. He's regarded as amongst the finest lyric poets in the English language. Some of his best know works include *To a Skylark*, *Ode to the West Wind* and *Ozymandias*.

These 'cutlets' are made with diced lobster meat with mushrooms, covered with meat glaze and set in a cutlet mould with pike forcemeat. They are then egged, crumbed and fried. The dish was created by Charles Ranhofer of Delmonico's Restaurant in New York, who presumably thought that a seafood dish was the best way to honour the great poet who had drowned in the sea off the coast of Italy at the age of 29.

SAUCES

Béarnaise Sauce

'I want there to be no peasant in my kingdom so poor that he cannot have a chicken in his pot every Sunday.'

There are various origin stories for this world famous sauce (egg yolks, vinegar and butter), though it can be agreed that it was named for the French king, **Henri IV** (1553–1610), who was known as *'le Grand Béarnais'*.

Some credit chef Jean-Louis-François Collinet, the inventor of puffed potatoes (*pommes de terre soufflées**), who served it at the 1836 opening of Le Pavillon Henri IV, his restaurant at Saint-Germain-en-Laye, not far from Paris. That Henri IV, himself a great gourmet, was born in the province of Béarn, only reinforces this evidence.

---

* *Pommes soufflés* were invented by chance on 24th August 1837, the opening day of the railway line between Paris, Gare Saint-Lazare and St-Germain-en- Laye. A reception had been arranged at the restaurant for Queen Marie-Amélie, who was arriving on the new line. As the train was delayed, Collinet had to reheat his fried potatoes by returning them to hot oil...to produce *pommes soufflées*.

Other sources suggest, however, that it was invented by the chef Jules Colette, who was from Béarn. He worked at Le Pavillon Henri IV for a time. Supposedly he had perfected the recipe long before he came to work at this restaurant.

It seems that every chef at the restaurant tried to claim the recipe as his own...

Recipe

(From *Bull Cook and Authentic Historical Recipes and Practices*, by George Leonard Herter)

Every good cook should be able to make a good **Béarnaise Sauce**. Here is the original recipe.

Take a small sauce pan or frying pan. Put into it one level teaspoon of grated spring onions or shallots or one level teaspoon of onion powder, one fourth teaspoon of white pepper, one level teaspoon of salt, two level teaspoons of dried tarragon leaves, rub the leaves well before adding them and remove any stem pieces, 2 drops of oil of anise and four level tablespoons of vinegar. Heat over a low flame until about one third of the vinegar goes off in steam. Stir well while this is going on, then remove the pan from the heat and leave to cool a little. Take five egg yolks and beat them together well in a bowl with a fork. Add the five beaten egg yolks gradually to the mixture in the pan stirring constantly and vigorously. Put the pan back on the stove over a very low fire and gradually add about six ounces of melted butter, stirring it in well. Do not let the sauce more than simmer. Be sure that the butter is just liquid and warm, not too hot as it is added. Stir the butter in well until the sauce is as thick as double cream. The egg yolks cooking causes the sauce to thicken. Remove the sauce just as soon as it thickens well and leave it to cool slightly. Serve it just slightly warm or even cold. Never serve it hot.

Béarnaise Sauce never contains wine, chervil, tarragon vinegar, nor cayenne pepper. It never is strained through a cloth or sieve as this changes the texture of the sauce entirely.

Béarnaise Sauce is best served on hamburgers. Cover both sides of the hamburger bun heavily with Béarnaise Sauce. Put lettuce on the hamburger and tomato, and dill pickle slices on it too if you like them. The Béarnaise Sauce makes a hamburger a fabulously different dish. In France, Béarnaise Sauce is served with roast beef or with such fish as halibut. You dip your pieces of roast beef into the Béarnaise Sauce instead of in gravy. It is really good and a welcome change every so often for anyone.

Served with fish instead of Tartar Sauce, Béarnaise Sauce is very good. It is excellent with fried fish or with cold fish like salmon or tuna. It makes a wonderful cracker dip.

Béchamel Sauce

The original **Béchamel Sauce** was invented by Duke Philippe De Mornay, governor of Saumur, Lord of Plessis Marly. He also invented **Mornay Sauce** (see page 225), Sauce Chasseur, Sauce Lyonnaise and Sauce Porto. Béchamel was subsequently named for **Louis de Béchamel, Marquis de Nointel** (1630–1703). Béchamel was a financier who held the honorary post of chief steward to Louis XIV.

Almost invariably persons who write or talk about Béchamel Sauce actually have no idea at all what they are talking about. They copy the recipe book, the author of which likewise did not know the true recipe either, and just make bad guesses. Even the so-called finest cook books do not have the true Béchamel Sauce recipes. Escoffier's Béchamel was terrible. Alexandre Dumas, who was a poor cook and knew little about cooking, in his book *Dictionary of the Cuisine*, never bothered to write the truth about cooking but simply wrote what he thought would make a book that would sell. His Béchamel recipe was entirely different from that of Escoffier and Escoffier's different from everyone else's.

Recipe

(From *Bull Cook and Authentic Historical Recipes and Practices*, by George Leonard Herter)

The original Béchamel Sauce invented by Mornay is as follows:

Put five level tablespoons of butter into a pan and melt over low heat. Do not brown. Remove the pan from heat. Add five level tablespoons of flour and stir in well with the butter but do not brown. Add one and three quarters cups of cold milk. Remember, cold milk. Warm milk will make the mixture lumpy. Put back on stove over medium heat. Stir well and bring to slow boil until the mixture thickens, add salt and pepper to taste and then quickly remove from heat. This is also sometimes called a white roux.

To make Brown Béchamel Sauce, make just the same but leave the butter to brown slightly before adding the flour. This is also sometimes called a Brun-Roux.

These basic Béchamel Sauces are the general basis for many sauces and soufflés. Béchamel Sauce in itself is not used alone at all, as some cooks would try to make you believe. Béchamel Sauce contains no cream, chicken stock, veal stock, onion, thyme or nutmeg.

Caruso Sauce

Caruso Sauce was created in the 1950s by Raymond Monti at the restaurant Mario & Alberto, in Montevideo, Uruguay. It included cream, sliced onions, cheese, nuts, and mushrooms. It is usually served with pasta, most often capelletti. A recipe from *A Year of Wine* has butter, flour, milk, salt, nutmeg, cinnamon, toasted walnuts and diced ham.

It commemorated the South American tours of legendary Italian operatic tenor **Enrico Caruso** (1873–1921) in the 1910s.

Choron Sauce

Choron Sauce is a variation on the classic **Béarnaise Sauce** (see page 214), made by adding tomato paste to the basic Béarnaise. Like Béarnaise, Choron Sauce is typically served with grilled steak.

Alexandre Etienne Choron (1837–1924) was *chef de cuisine* at the celebrated restaurant Voisin, in the rue Saint Honoré in Paris.

As well as for his sauce, Choron is also remembered for the dishes he served during the Siege of Paris by the Prussians, which began on 19th September 1870. During the siege, Parisians were reduced to eating cats, dogs, and rats. However, though the bourgeois continued to want to eat out in *de luxe* restaurants, they weren't happy eating such common animals. As the standard food reserves dwindled, the restaurants, including Voisin, had to improvise. Choron turned to the animals in the local zoo, and was soon serving a lot of exotic animal dishes at Voisin. For the midnight Christmas dinner of 1870,

Choron proposed a menu mainly composed of the best parts of the animals kept in the *Jardin d'acclimatation*: stuffed donkey's head, elephant consommé, roasted camel, kangaroo stew, bear shanks roasted in pepper sauce, wolf in deer sauce, cat with rat, and antelope in truffle sauce. The wines at the dinner must certainly have helped considerably to wash away any doubts in the diners' minds about what they were eating: Mouton-Rothschild 1846, Romanée-Conti 1858 and Château Palmer 1864.

Choron also became famous for his dishes containing elephant: *Trompe d'éléphant* in sauce chasseur and *Eléphant bourguignon*. After the elephant from the *Jardin d'acclimatation* graced the Christmas table, the two elephants (Castor and Pollux) at Paris's *Jardin zoologique* were consumed on 31st December 1870 at Voisin. In early January, it was the elephant at the *Jardin des Plantes* which was sent to the abattoir. It was bought by Choron for his restaurant at the price of 15 francs per pound. By 13th January, Voisin was out of elephant meat and substituted horse. The siege was lifted two weeks later.

Recipe

1 pint of Béarnaise Sauce
2 tablespoons of tomato paste

Cumberland Sauce

This was created in Germany in the late 19th century and named after the **Duke of Cumberland** (1845–1923), who had ties to Hanover in Germany. It is a complex version of a simple redcurrant sauce.

Despite its German origin, today the sauce is ubiquitous in the Cumbria region of England and is thought of as thoroughly British.

Recipe

Although variations do exist, common ingredients include redcurrants, port or wine, mustard, pepper, orange, ginger, and vinegar.

2½ cups of port
1 (10½ ounce) jar of red currant jelly
3 tablespoons of light brown sugar
2 tablespoons of grated orange rind
⅔ of a cup of fresh orange juice
1½ tablespoons of grated fresh ginger
2 teaspoons of dry mustard
¼ of a teaspoon of salt
¼ of a teaspoon of ground red pepper
2½ tablespoons of cornstarch

Bring 2 cups of port and the next 8 ingredients to a boil in a large saucepan, stirring constantly; reduce the heat, and simmer, stirring often for 20 minutes.

Stir together the remaining half cup of port and cornstarch until smooth. Stir into hot mixture; bring to a boil over medium heat. Boil, stirring constantly, for 1 minute. Remove from heat, and cool. Pour into hot sterilised jars, and seal. Store in the refrigerator for up to a month.

Makes about four cups.

Duxelles

A finely chopped mixture of mushrooms or mushroom stems, onions, shallots and herbs, sautéed in butter, and reduced to a paste (sometimes cream is used, as well).

Duxelles is said to have been created by the 17th-century French chef François Pierre La Varenne (1615–78), and to have been named after his employer **Nicolas Chalon du Blé, marquis d'Uxelles**.

It is a basic preparation used in stuffings and sauces (notably **Beef Wellington**, see page 102) or as a garnish. Duxelles can also be filled into a pocket of raw pastry and baked as a savoury tart.

It is made with any cultivated or wild mushroom, depending on the recipe. Duxelles made with porcini mushrooms will be much stronger flavoured than one made with white or brown mushrooms.

Many classical cookery books define Duxelles as dehydrated mushrooms, used as stuffings and pastry fillings. According to Auguste Escoffier, the mushrooms were dehydrated for the sole purpose of flavouring and minimising the water content. Once mushrooms are cooked, they let off enormous amounts of vapour in relation to their size, which would cause pressure inside the dish or pastry if they are not dehydrated, causing it to crack, or in extreme cases as with stuffing, explode.

Sauce Mirepoix

Sauce Mirepoix is a combination of diced carrots, onions and celery sautéed in butter and used as an aromatic base to flavour sauces, soups and stews. Even a small amount can significantly contribute to the overall flavour of a finished dish.

Gaston Pierre de Lévis (1699–1757), known as the '*duc de Lévis-Mirepoix*', marshall of France and ambassador of Louis XV, was a member of an ancient house that had been established in Languedoc as seigneurs of Mirepoix, since the 11th century.

According to Pierre Larousse (quoted in the *Oxford Companion to Food*), the unfortunate Duke was 'an incompetent and mediocre individual...who owed his vast fortune to the affection Louis XV felt toward his wife, and who had but one claim to fame: he gave his name to a sauce made of all kinds of meat and a variety of seasonings'.

Recipe

(From My Gourmet Connection)

The traditional Sauce Mirepoix recipe calls for two parts onion to one part each of celery and carrot.

If the Mirepoix is intended for brown stocks, sauces or stews, a small quantity of tomato paste is frequently added for colour and flavour. For white sauces, parsnip (or leek) is generally substituted for the carrot.

It is important to dice the vegetables as uniformly as possible to ensure even cooking. The size of the dice can vary according to overall cooking time of the dish for which it is intended. The shorter the cooking time the smaller the dice.

Cooking the vegetables in butter over a relatively low heat until they start to give off their juices and the onion to turn translucent is called 'sweating'. If you cover your pan during cooking, the process is then called 'smothering'.

For rich flavour and deep colour, prepare your Mirepoix as follows:

Start your onions and carrots first and cook them until they begin to brown. Add the celery and continue cooking until it softens and its colour becomes a brighter green. Stir in a small amount of tomato paste and cook until the entire mixture develops a rich brown colour. This technique is known as '*pinçage*'.

Sauce Mornay

A **Sauce Mornay** is a **Béchamel Sauce** (see page 217) with grated cheese added. Usually, it consists of half Gruyère and half parmesan. Some variations use different combinations of Gruyère, Emmental, or Cheddar.

It is often served with seafood or vegetables.

Philippe de Mornay (1549–1623), seigneur du Plessis Marly, was a French Protestant writer and member of the anti-monarchist *Monarchomaques*.

During the French Wars of Religion in 1567, he joined the army of Louis I de Bourbon, Prince de Condé, but a fall from his horse prevented him from taking an active part in the campaign.

He escaped the Saint Bartholomew's Day Massacre with the help of a Catholic friend, taking refuge in England. Returning to France towards the end of 1573, he participated during the next two years with various successes in the campaigns of the future Henri IV of France, then only King of Navarre. He was taken prisoner by the Duke of Guise on 10th October 1575, but ransomed for a small sum, which was paid by Charlotte Arbaleste, whom he married shortly afterwards.

Mornay was gradually recognised as Henri's right-hand man, representing him in England from 1577–78 and again in 1580, and in the Low Countries from 1581–82. With the death of the Duke of Alençon-Anjou in 1584, by which Henri was brought within sight of the throne of France, the period of Mornay's greatest political activity began, and after the death of the Prince of Condé in 1588, his influence became so great that he was popularly styled the 'Huguenot pope'.

From 1591–92, he was sent on a mission to the court of Queen Elizabeth I. Both he and his wife befriended English Protestants like Francis Walsingham, Mary Sidney, and her brother Philip Sydney.

His last years were saddened by the loss of his only son in 1605 and that of his devoted wife in 1606, but he spent them in perfecting the Huguenot organisation. He lost the governorship of Saumur at the time of the Huguenot insurrection in 1621 as Saumur was captured by French royal forces. He died in retirement on his estate of La Forêt-sur-Sèvre, Deux-Sèvres.

Soubise Purée

Soubise Purée is named for **Charles de Rohan, duke of Rohan-Rohan** (1715–87), seigneur of Roberval, and marshal of France from 1758, a military man, and a minister to kings Louis XV and Louis XVI. He was the last male of his branch of the House of Rohan. He was also great-grandfather to the duc d'Enghien, executed by Napoleon in 1804. Styled '*prince d'Epinoy*' at birth, on his father's death in 1724 he became the Prince of Soubise.

Recipe

White onions are well boiled but not coloured. Then cooked white rice is added. Together they are cooked further before being passed through a very fine sieve. Finally butter and seasonings are added. There also exists the Sauce Soubise, which is a Soubise Purée added to a **Béchamel Sauce** (see page 217), mixed well with whipping cream.

Sauce Véron

See **Fillets of Brill Véron**, page 188.

Recipe

Prepare a reduced herb mixture as for a **Béarnaise Sauce** (see page 214). Then add 7 fluid ounces of Normande Sauce (fish fumet, mushroom essence, eggs) and 2 tablespoons of very concentrated brown veal stock or fish glaze. Season with a pinch of cayenne pepper, rub through a sieve and finally add 1 tablespoon of snipped chervil or tarragon.

VEGETABLES

~

Potatoes Anna

(Pommes Anna)

The most famous dish attributed to the chef Adolphe Dugléré is almost certainly **Potatoes Anna**. Although he never confirmed which lady it was, it was almost certainly either the actress **Anna Judic**, whose real name was Anne Marie-Louis Damiens, or rather more probably **Anna Deslions**, a 19th-century Parisian celebrity and member of the world's oldest profession (*grande cocotte*), although she certainly didn't see herself that way, as it is said that she never charged her clients. She merely accepted trinkets such as diamonds and beautiful apartments from them. Her favourite meeting place was the famous Café des Anglais, and it seems that she brought much royal, imperial and aristocratic business to the restaurant by way of her guests. No wonder Dugléré saw fit to create and name a dish in her honour.

Sadly though, Dugléré didn't leave one single cookery book, so the authentic recipe for Pommes Anna is uncertain. It did, however, very rapidly became a classic, and other authors of cookery books made sure they included it.

Recipe

(From *The Epicurean*, by Charles Ranhofer)

Choose long-shaped potatoes; they must be peeled and cut into the form of a large cork; slice them finely, and soak the slices in water for a few moments; drain and wipe them on a cloth. Butter the inside of a thick copper pan, having a well-fitted cover; arrange on the bottom and sides a thin layer of the potatoes, one overlapping the other, then fill entirely with the remaining ones in separate layers, covering each with softened butter, free from moisture; mask the upper layer with the same, and close with the lid. Cook the potatoes for three-quarters of an hour in the oven; a quarter of an hour before serving take from the fire, drain off the butter and cut a cross through the potatoes still in the pan, and turn each quarter over with the aid of a palette; put back the drained-off butter and return to the oven until ready, and invert on a dish to serve. These potatoes may be made in a smaller pan; in this case they should not be cut but turned over whole before putting in the oven a second time.

Beet Fritters à la Dickens

(Beignets de betteraves à la Dickens)

Named for **Charles Dickens** by Charles Ranhofer of Delmonico's in New York.

See **Veal Pie à la Dickens**, page 106.

Recipe

(From *The Epicurean*, by Charles Ranhofer)

Cut some beetroots cooked as below in slices, each one an eighth of an inch thick; wipe dry and put on half of them a quarter of an inch thick layer of the following preparation: Fry two well-chopped onions colourless in butter; add four ounces of chopped mushrooms and a pinch of minced chervil, salt and pepper; on this layer place another round of beetroot, and from the whole remove rounds an inch and a half in diameter; dip these in frying batter and plunge into very hot frying fat, drain, wipe and dress as a garnishing around a meat remove.

Potatoes Christian Herter

These potatoes were invented by Berthe Herter, wife of George Leonard Herter, for the couple's son **Christian**, and there is just nothing like them nor any form of potatoes as good as they are. The only trouble with them is they simply take too long to prepare. Use them only when you really want to put someone in his place who does not think too much of your cooking.

Recipe

(From *Bull Cook and Authentic Historical Recipes and Practices*, by George Leonard Herter)

Make a suitable sized batch of mashed potatoes. Use the desired amount of milk or cream to give them the proper consistency and plenty of butter. Now for about every four cups of mashed potatoes add a quarter-level teaspoon of ground nutmeg and a 4-ounce can or jar of pimentos chopped up real fine or grated real fine. Add the liquid the pimentos came packed in also. Mix well into the mashed potatoes and add salt and pepper to taste.

Make a batch of hollow French-fried soufflé potatoes. When done, carefully cut a flap in one end of each soufflé potato and with your little finger stuff each one with the mashed potato, nutmeg and pimento mixture. Keep them warm in an oven until served. This is going all out on potatoes but well worth the effort on real special occasions.

Jansson's Temptation

It has often been claimed that the name for this potato dish originated with the Swedish opera singer **Per Adolf 'Pelle' Janzon** (1844–89), remembered as a gourmand. However, another claim has been made by Gunnar Stigmark in an article in the periodical *Gastronomisk kalender*. According to Stigmark, the name was borrowed from the 1928 film *Janssons frestelse*, which featured the popular actor Edvin Adolphson. The name for the dish was coined by Stigmark's mother on the occasion of a society dinner, whence it spread to other households and eventually into cookery books.

Recipe

The potatoes are cut into thin slices and layered in a roasting tin, alternating with the sprats and chopped onions. Salt and pepper is put over each layer, then cream is added so that it almost fills the tin. It is finally baked in an oven at 200 °C (392 °F) for about one hour.

The recipe is often understandably mistranslated into English, with anchovies being substituted for sprats. This is because, since the middle of the 19th century, sprats pickled in sugar, salt and spices have been known in Sweden as *anjovis*, while true anchovies are sold in Sweden as *sardeller*.

Small herrings may be used instead of sprats.

Potatoes O'Brien

Potato chips fried with diced green peppers.

One source has it that the naming of this dish was simply because **O'Brien** was a typical Irish name and Ireland is very much associated with potatoes. However, *The Old Foodie* suggests that the honour goes by default almost to the only person found with that name to have a significant association with potatoes, **William Smith O'Brien** (1803–64), the Irish nationalist and leader of a post-famine revolt, who was eventually transported to Australia.

Potatoes Parmentier

Diced potatos, shallow-fried in butter and finished with chopped parsley.

In 1748, the French parliament forbade the cultivation of potatoes; they were thought to cause leprosy as well as fevers. Twenty-four years later, however, in 1772, the Paris Faculty of Medicine declared that potatoes were edible.

A key figure in the saga of France and the potato was **Antoine-Augustin Parmentier** (1737–1813), Monsieur – later Monsieur le Baron – Parmentier. During the Seven Years' War, Parmentier served as an army pharmacist, but was captured by the Prussians and imprisoned in Westphalia. There the potato was highly prized by the locals, and there too Parmentier discovered its nutritional value.

Parmentier returned to Paris in 1763 where he continued his pioneering work in nutritional chemistry. In 1772 the Academy of Besançon offered a prize for the discovery of plants likely to be of use to man in the case of famine. Parmentier won the prize in 1773. There was a famine in 1785.

Ultimately, Louis XVI recognised Parmentier's work by saying: 'France will thank you some day for having found bread for the poor'. In fact, he is best honoured by the pleasure his country takes in making and eating **Potage Parmentier** (see page 236).

Parmentier also managed the first mandatory smallpox vaccination campaign (under Napoleon), and he was a pioneer of the extraction of sugar from sugar beet. As well, he founded a school of bread making and studied methods of conserving food (including refrigeration), cheese making, grain storage, maize and chestnut flour, mushroom culture, mineral waters, wine making, etc...

Vegetables Rachel

Artichoke bases with bone marrow and parsley, dressed with a Bordelaise Sauce.

See **Salade Rachel**, page 57, **Tournedos Rachel**, page 95, **Eggs Rachel**, page 174, **Filet de Sole Rachel**, page 187, and the **Rachel Sandwich**, page 258.

Mashed Potatoes
Anne Phoebe Charlton Key Taney

Mashed potatoes prepared properly are one of the best-tasting foods known to mankind. **Anne Phoebe Charlton Key Taney** (1783–1855) was the sister of Francis Key, the lawyer. He immortalised himself by immortalising the famous English naval attack on Fort McHenry (September 13th/14th, 1814) through the song he wrote entitled *The Star Spangled Banner*. Anne Key was a very beautiful woman. On 7th January 1806 she married Roger Brooke Taney, a man who had gone to law school with her brother. Anne had seven fine children about as rapidly as possible and was a pretty busy woman. She found time, however, to vastly improve on the cooking methods of her time. I believe that her greatest contribution to good cooking was the method she devised for mashing potatoes. Here is her original method.

Recipe

(From *Bull Cook and Authentic Historical Recipes and Practices*, by George Leonard Herter)

Peel your potatoes and boil them until well done. Remove and put in a bowl to mash them in. Add about one-fourth level teaspoon of baking powder per two cups of potatoes. Mash the potatoes, mixing in the baking power well. Now add just sufficient milk or cream to give the potatoes the consistency you desire and mash them well. Put in a serving bowl and sprinkle the top of the potatoes quite heavily with paprika. The baking powder keeps the potatoes snowy white and fluffy. Even any leftover mashed potatoes will be white and fluffy the next day. If you freeze the mashed potatoes made with this method, they will still remain white and tasty.

Celery Victor

Victor Hirtzler (1875–1935) was head chef at the St Francis Hotel in San Francisco.

Recipe

Wash six stalks of large celery. Make a stock with one soup hen or chicken bones, and five pounds of veal bones, in the usual manner, with carrots, onions, bay leaves, parsley, salt and whole pepper. Place celery in vessel and strain broth over same, and boil until soft. Allow to cool in the broth. When cold press the broth out of the celery gently with the hands, and place on a plate. Season with salt, fresh ground black pepper, chervil, and one-quarter white wine tarragon vinegar to three-quarters of olive oil.

Woolton Pie

Woolton Pie, at first known as **Lord Woolton pie**, was an adaptable dish of vegetables created in 1941 at the Savoy Hotel in London by its then *maître chef de cuisine*, Francis Latry. It was one of a number of recipes commended to the British public by the Ministry of Food during the Second World War to enable a nutritional diet to be maintained, despite shortages and rationing of many types of food, especially meat.

It was named after **Frederick Marquis, 1st Lord Woolton** (1883–1964), who became Minister of Food in 1940.

PUDDINGS

~

Bananas Alexander the Great

'There is nothing impossible to him who will try.'

Alexander the Great, Alexander III of Macedonia (356–323 BC), 'Lord of Asia', 'Pharaoh of Egypt', was one of the greatest military geniuses of all time. At the age of 12 he tamed the horse he was to ride in all his major battles, the unruly stallion Bucephalus.

Also aged 12, he pushed his teacher Nectanebus into a pit and killed him. Maybe present day teenagers are not so bad after all.

Alexander in his conquests in India saw banana trees for the first time. He had bananas prepared for him with the following recipe, and it is, I believe, the finest banana recipe ever invented.

Recipe

Take a bowl of fresh whole milk. Add one level tablespoon of honey. Stir the honey into the milk until it is dissolved. This takes quite a bit of time as honey doesn't dissolve easily. Then slice a banana into the honey flavoured milk and eat at once.

This recipe makes fabulously good eating.

Charlotte Russe

A Bavarian cream in a charlotte mould lined with sponge fingers, these often soaked in coffee or a liqueur.

This was invented by Antoine Carême. There is some doubt about the origin of the name 'charlotte'. Despite the fact that charlottes are found all over Europe, one etymology suggests that it's a corruption of the Old English word *charlyt* meaning 'a dish of custard'. Another possibility is that it took its name from **Queen Charlotte** (1744–1818), the wife of the British king George III. A third possibility is Alexander I of Russia's sister-in-law, **Charlotte of Prussia**. The 'Russe', in this case, may then refer to the Tsar himself.

Peach Pudding à la Cleveland

Grover Cleveland (1837–1908) was both the 22nd and 24th US President, and indeed the only person to have held that office for two non-consecutive terms.

In a letter to a friend, Cleveland once wrote, 'I must go to dinner. I wish it was to eat a pickled herring, Swiss cheese and a chop at Louis' instead of the French stuff I shall find.' But this known preference for simplicity didn't stop the chef Charles Ranhofer from naming this rich French pudding, made with 20 peaches macerated in powdered sugar and topped with a Madeira Sauce, after the president.

Bananas Foster

This (from *Brennan's New Orleans Cookbook*) is made with brown sugar, butter, cinnamon, banana, banana liqueur, white rum and vanilla cream. It was created in 1951 by Paul Blangé, the chef at Brennan's Restaurant in New Orleans and named by the owner of the restaurant, Owen Brennan, after his good friend and regular customer, **Richard Foster**.

Apricots with Rice à la Jefferson

Apricots with Rice à la Jefferson, named for **Thomas Jefferson** (1743–1826), 3rd US President, was another creation by Charles Ranhofer, the 19th-century chef at New York's famed Delmonico's restaurant, who named dozens of dishes after his celebrity clientele. However, he reached back in history to name this rice pudding.

Humbolt Pudding

This is an elaborate moulded pudding made with pancakes, apricot marmalade, almonds, eggs, sugar, corn syrup and Madeira. It is named after the Prussian geographer, explorer and naturalist, **Friedrich Wilhelm Heinrich Alexander von Humboldt** (1769–1859). Apart from the pudding, 11 species, 14 geographical features, 36 places and 25 universities, colleges or schools are named after him, perhaps most notably, the prestigious Humboldt University in Berlin.

Kaiserschmarrn

This, to English ears at least, is not a very appetising sounding dish.

Kaiserschmarrn (or Kaiserschmarren) is a shredded pancake, named after the Austrian emperor **Kaiser Franz Joseph I of Austria** (1830–1916), who was very fond of this kind of fluffy shredded pancake. It is popular Austria, South Germany, Hungary, Slovenia, and northern Croatia.

The name 'Kaiserschmarrn' is a compound of the words '*Schmarren*' (shredded pancake) and '*Kaiser*' (emperor). *Schmarren* is a colloquialism used in Austria and Bavaria to mean 'trifle, mishmash, mess, nonsense and folly'. It is related to '*scharren*' (to scrape) and '*schmieren*' (to smear). The Kaiser's love for this dish was referred to humorously as his 'folly'.

One apocryphal story involves the Kaiser and his wife, Elisabeth of Bavaria. Obsessed with maintaining her minimal waistline, the Empress Elisabeth directed the royal chef to prepare only light desserts for her, much to the consternation and annoyance of her notoriously austere husband. Upon being presented with the chef's confection, she found it too rich and refused to eat it. The exasperated Franz Joseph quipped, 'Now let me see what 'Schmarren' our chef has cooked up.' It apparently met with his approval; he finished his and even his wife's serving. Thereafter, across the Empire, the dessert was called 'Kaiserschmarrn'.

Recipe

It is made from a sweet batter using flour, eggs, sugar, salt, and milk, baked in butter. When making Kaiserschmarrn, the egg whites are usually separated from the yolk and beaten until stiff; then the flour and the yolks are mixed with sugar, and the other ingredients added. These can include nuts, cherries, plums, apple jam, or small pieces of apple, or caramelised raisins and slivered almonds. These aren't in the original recipe but are additions made by some cooks based on their personal preferences. In the original recipe there are only raisins soaked in rum before cooking.

The pancake is split with two forks into pieces while frying and usually sprinkled with powdered sugar, then served hot with apple or plum sauce or various fruit compotes, including plum, lingonberry, strawberry, or apple. Kaiserschmarrn is eaten as a dessert, or eaten for lunch at tourist places like mountainside restaurants and taverns in the Austrian Alps. It can be quite filling.

Peach Melba

These are named for the world-famous Australian soprano, **Dame Nellie Melba** (1861–1931).

In 1892, Melba was performing in Wagner's opera *Lohengrin* at Covent Garden. To celebrate her triumph in the opera, her then lover, Philippe, Duke of Orléans gave a dinner party in her honour at the Savoy Hotel. For the occasion, the hotel's renowned chef Escoffier created a new dessert of peaches and raspberry sauce with vanilla ice cream. To display it, he used an ice sculpture of a swan (a swan features in the opera). The swan carried the peaches which rested on a bed of vanilla ice cream and which were topped with spun sugar.

In 1900 Escoffier created a new version of the dessert. This was for the opening of the Carlton Hotel, where he was now head chef. He omitted the ice swan and topped the peaches with raspberry purée.

See **Melba Toast**, page 18.

Marshal Ney

Created by Charles Ranhofer, a **Marsahl Ney** consists of moulded tiers of meringue shells, vanilla custard, and marzipan. This dessert is named after Napoleon's marshal **Michel Ney** (1769–1815), who led the retreat from Moscow and was a commander at Waterloo. Following Napoleon's defeat at Waterloo in 1815, he was executed under the new Bourbon regime as an example to the fallen emperor's other commanders, many of whom had been exonerated.

Strawberries Romanoff

(Fraises Romanoff)

The **House of Romanov** was the second and last imperial dynasty to rule over Russia, reigning from 1613 until 1917, when the February Revolution abolished the crown.

Antoine Carême created **Fraises Romanoff** for Tsar Alexander I (1777–1825). It is probably more French than Russian, but appears in the cookery books of both countries.

Not surprisingly there is also an American contender to being the inventor of Strawberries Romanoff; the self-styled **Prince Michael Romanoff**.

Michael Romanoff (1890–1971), born Hershel Geguzin, and alternately known as Harry F. Gerguson and Prince Michael Dimitri Aleandrovich Obolensky-Romanoff, was a Hollywood restaurateur, actor and conman, born in Lithuania. He is perhaps best remembered as the owner of the now-defunct Romanoff's restaurant in Beverly Hills, popular with Hollywood stars in the 1940s and 1950s. It closed on New Year's Eve 1962.

The main difference between the Russian, French and American recipes for Strawberries Romanoff is in which liqueur is used. The Russian one uses Cointreau, the French Curaçao and the American Grand Marnier.

Soufflé Rothschild

Antoine Carême's invention of the classic soufflé in the early 1820s was made possible by new ovens, which were heated by air drafts instead of by coal. This provided the more even cooking temperature needed for a soufflé to rise properly and stay risen. Initially, Carême made his soufflés in stiff pastry casings that were not eaten. Their straight sides were the inspiration for our current soufflé dishes. Carême went on to create hundreds of other soufflés, including the **Soufflé Rothschild**, which originally contained real gold and was aptly named by its creator in honour of his employer, the notable French banker and diplomat, **Baron de Rothschild** (1792–1868), at the time the richest man in France.

It consisted of a pastry-cream base lightened with beaten egg whites and flavoured with chopped crystallized fruits macerated in Danziger Goldwasser, a liquor containing flecks of gold. It was served surrounded with fresh strawberries.

Crêpes Suzette

Henri Charpentier (1880–1961) was a Frenchman who became John D. Rockefeller's chef in America. In his autobiography *Life à la Henri*, Charpentier describes how, at the age of 14, when he was working at the Café de Paris in Monte Carlo, he created **Crêpes Suzette** for **Edward, Prince of Wales** (later Edward VIII):

'It was quite by accident as I worked in front of a chafing dish that the cordials caught fire. I thought I was ruined. The Prince and his friends were waiting. How could I begin all over?

I tasted it. It was, I thought, the most delicious melody of sweet flavours I had ever tasted. I still think so. That accident of the flame was precisely what was needed to bring all those various instruments into one harmony of taste…

He ate the pancakes with a fork; but he used a spoon to capture the remaining syrup. He asked me the name of that which he had eaten with so much relish. I told him it was to be called *Crêpes Princesse*. He recognized that the pancake controlled the gender and that this was a compliment designed for him; but he protested with mock ferocity that there was a lady present.* She was alert and rose to her feet and holding her little skirt wide with her hands she made him a curtsey. "Will you," said His Majesty, "change *Crêpes Princesse* to *Crêpes Suzette?*" Thus was born and baptized this confection, one taste of which, I really believe, would reform a cannibal into a civilized gentleman. The next day I received a present from the Prince, a jewelled ring, a panama hat and a cane.'

Tarte Tatin

Tradition says that the **Tarte Tatin** was first created in 1898, by accident, at a hotel in Lamotte-Beuvron in France. The hotel was run by two sisters, **Stéphanie** (1838–1917) and **Caroline** (1847–1911) **Tatin**.

There are conflicting accounts of the *Tarte*'s origin, but the

---

* Very possibly the daughter of Edward's (unnamed) host.'

predominant one is that Stéphanie, who did most of the cooking, was overworked one day. She started to make a traditional apple pie but left the apples cooking in butter and sugar for too long. Smelling burning, she tried to rescue the dish by sticking the pastry base on top of the pan of apples, and quickly finishing the cooking by putting the whole pan in the oven. After turning out the upside-down tart, she was surprised to find how much the hotel guests appreciated the pudding.

In an alternative version, Stéphanie simply baked a caramelised apple tart upside-down by mistake. Regardless, she served her guests the unusual dish hot from the oven and a classic was born.

Yet another version says that Stéphanie was chatting up, or being chatted up by, a guest at the hotel…

The *Tarte* became a speciality at the hotel and the recipe spread through the Sologne region. Its lasting fame is probably due to the restaurateur Louis Vaudable (1902–83), who tasted it on a visit to the Sologne and made it a permanent fixture on the menu at his restaurant in Paris, Maxim's.

Nowadays in Lamotte-Beuvron, what used to be called the Hôtel de la Gare is not surprisingly called the Hôtel Tatin. I stayed there once, and apart from the Tarte Tatin, my strongest memory is of the truly hideous wallpaper in my bedroom.*

---

* Oscar Wilde's last words are often said to have been his comment on the awful wallpaper in his room at the HOtel d'Alsace in Paris – 'One of us had to go…'

The original stove in which the first Tartes Tatin were made is in the hotel foyer. It looked either as if it has just been delivered and was about to be installed in the kitchen, or, more likely, considering its age, as if it had just been disconnected and moved out of the kitchen and was waiting to be taken away.

In spite of looking very out of place in the foyer, this is where it lives and where it is staying.

Washington Pie

This was named after the first American president, **George Washington** (1732–99). It is a light custardy confection similar to a Boston Cream Pie, but with additional layers of raspberry jam inside and a sprinkling of confectioner's sugar on top.

A Boston Cream Pie is a cake filled with a custard or cream filling and frosted with chocolate. Although it's called a Boston Cream Pie, it is in fact a cake.

SANDWICHES

Hot Brown Sandwich

A **Hot Brown Sandwich** (sometimes known as a Kentucky Hot Brown) is an American hot sandwich originally created at the **Brown Hotel** in Louisville, Kentucky, by Fred K. Schmidt in 1926. It was created to serve as an alternative to ham and egg late-night suppers.

The Hot Brown is an open-faced sandwich of turkey and bacon, covered in **Mornay Sauce** (see page 225) and baked or grilled until the bread is crisp and the sauce has begun to brown. Many Hot Browns also include ham with the turkey, and either pimentos or tomatoes on top of the sauce.

Elvis Sandwich

A sandwich containing peanut butter, banana, bacon.
À *chacun son goût…*

Elvis Presley (1935–77) was a legendary rock and roll singer, also known as 'The King'. Depending on where you look, and on whether you count private recordings and rehearsals, the number of songs sung and recorded by Elvis varies between 500 and 1,000.

Reuben Sandwich

Though several variants exist, the original **Reuben Sandwich** is generally thought to be a hot sandwich with corned beef, Swiss cheese, Russian dressing, and sauerkraut. These are made with rye bread and grilled.

One account holds that **Reuben Kulakofsky** (1874–1960), a Lithuanian-born grocer in Omaha, Nebraska, was the inventor of the Reuben Sandwich, perhaps as part of a group effort by members of Kulakofsky's weekly poker game at the Blackstone Hotel from around 1920 to 1935. The participants, who nicknamed themselves 'the committee', included the hotel's owner, Charles Schimmel. The sandwich first gained local fame when Schimmel put it on the Blackstone's lunch menu. Its fame spread when a former employee of the hotel won a national contest with the recipe.

Another account holds that the Reuben's creator was **Arnold Reuben** (1883–1970), the German owner of the famed, yet now defunct Reuben's Delicatessen in New York City. According to an interview with Craig Claiborne, Arnold Reuben invented the 'Reuben Special' around 1914. The earliest reference to it in is in a 1926 edition of *Theatre Magazine*, which does seem to take its cue from Arnold Reuben's menu.

Yet another version of the above account is related by Bernard Sobel in his book *Broadway Heartbeat: Memoirs of a Press Agent*, which claims that the sandwich was an extemporaneous creation for the famed Broadway actress Marjorie Rambeau when she visited the Reuben's Delicatessen one night when the cupboards were particularly bare. Some sources say the actress was Annette Seelos, not Marjorie Rambeau. They also note that the original Reuben Special didn't contain corned beef or sauerkraut and wasn't grilled. Still other versions give credit to Reuben's chef Alfred Scheuing, and say he created the sandwich for Reuben's son **Arnold Jr.** in the 1930s.

The **West Coast Reuben** is a variation on the standard Reuben Sandwich, substituting Dijon mustard as the dressing. This variation is often a menu item in restaurants in Las Vegas.

The **Montreal Reuben** substitutes Montreal smoked meat for corned beef.

The **Rachel Sandwich** (named for the ubiquitous **Mademoiselle Rachel**) is a variation on the standard Reuben Sandwich, substituting pastrami for the corned beef, and coleslaw for the sauerkraut. Yet other recipes for the Rachel call for turkey instead of corned beef or pastrami. In some parts of the United States, especially Michigan, this turkey variant is known as a **Georgia Reuben** or **California Reuben**, which sometimes uses Barbecue Sauce instead of Russian or Thousand Island.

See **Salade Rachel**, page 57, **Tournedos Rachel**, page 95, **Eggs Rachel**, page 174, **Filet de Sole Rachel**, page 187, and **Vegetable Rachel**, page 237.

Sandwich

John Montagu, 4th Earl of Sandwich (1718–92) is the originator of arguably the best and best known eponym ever.

Apparently Sandwich was a very enthusiastic gambler. During his long hours at the card table he didn't have time to have a meal, so would ask his servants to bring him slices of meat between two pieces of bread. This habit became well known among his gambling friends and, because Montagu also happened to be a fourth earl, others began to order 'the same as Sandwich!' Thus was born the **Sandwich**.

However, the exact circumstances of the invention are still the subject of debate. A sober alternative to the idea of a hungry gambling earl is provided by Sandwich's biographer N.A.M. Rodger, who suggested that Sandwich's commitments to the navy, to politics and to the arts meant the first sandwich was more likely to have been consumed at his desk.

The town of Sandwich in Kent, one of the Cinque Ports, used to be by the sea. But the sea has now receded leaving the town two miles inland.

The town is no stranger to odd events in English history. It was here in 1255 that the first captive elephant was landed in England. The prize beast arrived at Sandwich quayside, delivered from the French king Louis IX as a gift to the English monarch Henry III. It was then taken on foot to the king's zoo at the Tower of London. The journey through Kent is reported to have proceeded without incident, except for when a bull in a field next to the road took umbrage at the great beast passing and attacked it. In one move the bull was thrown by the elephant and killed outright.

The present earl at the time of writing is the 11th, John Edward Hollister Montagu, born 1943.

National Sandwich Week is held each year in the middle of May. I feel there ought to be a collective noun for sandwiches. Considering their history we could do a lot worse than an earl of sandwiches.

Finis

Acknowledgements

First of all, sincerest and humblest apologies to anyone I might have left out below, which hopefully, is no one.

Huge thanks to my late wife Suzie, not only for her love and encouragement but for her great patience, and also to the following who have helped in countless ways; in matters factual, stylistic and grammatical, and who not only spotted my silly mistakes but also suggested improvements and additions. Their enthusiasm helped very much indeed when mine was beginning to flag.

Timothy d'Arch Smith
Kate Dixey
Geoffrey Eathorne
Ed Glover
Ian Graham
Piers Hartley
Jon Harris
Kate Henry
Colin Hodson
Heather Holden-Brown

Cressida Luke
Ronni Lundy
Ruary and Kari Mackenzie Dodds
John and Caroline Molony
John P. Parke
Felix Pryor
Guy Pawson
Robert Raikes
Nicola Reid
Sir George and Lady Richmond Brown
Louise Rodden
Ron Rubin
Julia Trustram Eve
Richard and Celia Turner
David Villiers-Child
Ginny Vere Nicoll
Millie Wolsey

Last but by no means least may I thank my publisher Anthony Weldon who saw a book in half a dozen sample pages, and his colleague Dominic Horsfall who brilliantly and diplomatically edited my final manuscript.

More foodie books
by Robert Booth

Eating the Alphabet

An A–Z of curiosities from the world of food
Robert Booth

From A–Z (as is customary), Eating the Alphabet is a dictionary of the essential and the ridiculous relating to all things food and drink. People and inventions, recipes and their origins, vegetables and fine wines; all are served up and dissected to reveal the curiosities that we swallow up every day.

"The first Indian restaurant in London? What Balzac ate for dinner? Who invented the tin-opener? And was it kinky when the Prince of Wales (later George IV) said he preferred 'mutton dressed as lamb'? Robert Booth's wondrously eccentric Eating the Alphabet contains the diverting and wacky answers, plus a hundred other things both you and I didn't know about the subjects of food and drink."
Paul Levy, author, journalist and original 'foodie'

Hardback • ISBN: 978-1-909657-59-5 • Price: £9.99

Who's on the Bottle

Liquid curiosities uncorked
Robert Booth

Robert Booth celebrates all those who saw fit to add some wonder to the world by pouring their creative genius into a bottle. From fine wines to bottled water, and everything in between, we discover who we really should be toasting next time we raise our glasses. This is the perfect complement to Booth's previous title, **Who's on the Menu**, this time championing the drink creators instead of the foodies.

"*Robert Booth has written a splendid book about drink and drinkers. It is a delight from the first drop to when you swallow the last bit in your glass and decide to have another one. I lost count of the number of times I said to myself 'God, I never knew that!' An ideal companion for a quiet evening – preferably on your own and with a glass in your hand.*"
Henry Kelly

Hardback • ISBN: 978-1-909657-74-8 • Price: £9.99

Words of Food

A Feast of Fit and Wisdom
Robert Booth

Gastronomic enthusiast, Robert Booth, brings his collection of Words to the table, offering up the world of food and drink for quotation, and calling on the finest chefs, the proudest drinkers, and even those who can barely boil an egg, to talk with their mouths full and proffer their wisdom.

This compilation of quotations is unique in its variety and range of sources. From the gourmet to the serial snacker, there is something for everyone in the quest to laud and celebrate that most universal of pleasures: eating.

"One of the very nicest things about life is the way we must regularly stop whatever it is we are doing and devote our attention to eating."
Pavarotti

Hardback • ISBN: 978-1-903071-97-7 • Price: £9.99

Discover more great titles at

www.bene-factum.co.uk